On the
road to
emmaus

A TRAVEL GUIDE
THROUGH GRIEF

Myrlene Hamilton Hess

Foreword by William H. Griffith

JUDSON PRESS
PUBLISHERS SINCE 1824
VALLEY FORGE, PA

On the Road to Emmaus: A Travel Guide through Grief
© 2008 by Judson Press, Valley Forge, PA 19482-0851
All rights reserved.

The author and Judson Press have made every effort to trace the ownership of all quotes. In the event of a question arising from the use of a quote, we regret any error made and will be pleased to make the necessary correction in future printings and editions of this book.

Bible quotations in this volume are from the New Revised Standard Version Bible, copyright 1989, Division of Christian Education of the National Council of the Churches of Christ in the United States of America. Used by permission. All rights reserved.

Library of Congress Cataloging-in-Publication Data

Hamilton, Myrlene L. J., 1952-
On the road to Emmaus : a travel guide through grief / Myrlene Hamilton Hess.
   p. cm.
   Includes bibliographical references.
ISBN 978-0-8170-1533-6 (pbk. : alk. paper) 1. Grief—Religious aspects—
Christianity. 2. Spirituality. 3. Church work with the bereaved. I. Title.
   BV4905.3.H35   2008
   248.8'66— dc22

                                                                2008005900

Printed on recycled paper in the U.S.A.
First Edition, 2008.

For Eric,
with shared memories
of Ed and Adrianne

Contents

Foreword

Simply defined, grief is losing something we value. It is a life experience from which no one is exempt. In fact, it becomes a recurring emotion with a powerful way of distorting all of life. We begin to develop ways of coping with grief from our earliest years as children, and yet nowhere in our formal educational process are we taught how to deal with loss.

On the Road to Emmaus is a welcomed resource that helps readers discover their own way to work through grief. Part of that journey is confronting the reality of loss and exploring what the process of grieving looks like. The author emphasizes the importance of learning from others who are willing to share their stories of grief. Hearing another's story provides the listener the opportunity to see oneself in the story and learn from it. Isn't that why Jesus taught in parables? We often find it easier to hide (and find) ourselves in story than in a direct or didactic lesson.

The book's title itself references a story—the biblical story of two grieving disciples heading home to Emmaus after the crucifixion. Their experience of meeting Jesus along the way becomes the overarching metaphor for the book—encouraging us to make Jesus himself our travel companion along the road of our grief.

Myrlene Hamilton weaves her personal life story with those of others with whom she has traveled the "Emmaus road." In doing so, she encourages readers to reflect creatively on personal life experiences and to remember the feelings and emotions that grief brings. She provides insights into our grief by telling her own grief stories and by sharing the lessons she has learned from her continuing journey.

The author's personal stories include a wide range of grief experiences that begin with her experience of loss as a teenager, and then as an adult when her first husband died. She shares her feelings and struggles candidly, and from her honesty, readers become free to connect their own experiences with hers.

This is not a book to sit down and read through at one sitting. It is meant to be like the Global Positioning System (GPS) guide in a car. Along the Emmaus road, Hamilton pauses periodically to reflect on the meaning of the latest experience and to spell out for the reader the basic dynamics of the grief process. She invites the reader to pause with her and record personal reflections of where they are in their journey.

Because the author knows the importance of sharing the journey with others, she also provides excellent resources for groups to use in taking the journey together. In the appendix you'll find a participants' guide for use a bereavement support group. The leader's guide is available for free download on the publisher's website.

I have a wide variety of books on grief in my library, but this volume fills a particular gap among religious texts. *On the Road to Emmaus* is a resource that enables the Christian reader to travel the often lonely and winding road through grief with faith-filled confidence, knowing that the human author has navigated the same road and that Jesus continues to be a companion on the Emmaus road.

William H. Griffith
Pastor, chaplain, and author
*More Than a Parting Prayer: Lessons
in Care-giving for the Dying*

Acknowledgments

I would not have been able to write this book had it not been for the amazing and often intense years of marriage to Ed Hamilton, whose life *and* death inspired me. I am grateful for those years, and for the grace of God that brought us together, led us through twenty-two years of marriage and ministry, and still leads me now.

Thank you to Margie, Eric, Dan, Elaine, and Michelle, for having the courage and vulnerability to allow me to profile their grief journeys in this book.

I also want to thank my many companions on the road to Emmaus. I extend my gratitude to each one who has been a source of strength. Special thanks to Ruth Castellano, Mary Austin, Michelle Larsen, Bill Jordan, and of course . . . Eric, who walks with me and has given great encouragement in the writing of this book.

Great thanks, too, to the good folks at Judson Press, particularly my editor Rebecca Irwin-Diehl, for encouraging me in this pursuit.

How to Use This Book

I designed this book as a travel guide for those who are grieving. Think of yourself on a journey, with this book as a companion. I suggest that you partake of it in small bites. Each vignette is brief and meant to be a thought starter. I share observations from my own experience as well as the experience of people I have known. I also share knowledge from my study on the topic of grief. At the end of each vignette, I pose reflection questions (My Travel Journal) for you to mull over, pray about, or discuss in a group setting. Under Suggested Itinerary are practical suggestions (places to go, things to do) for working on your grief issues that relate to the specific topic of the vignette. You may also find it helpful to keep a journal. Jot down observations, questions, and feelings. After you've traveled down the road a ways, I recommend that you revisit those comments and consider how you've moved and grown. Consider all of this as an invitation to engage with your grief process. But please don't feel pressured to do it all. If you don't have time or are not ready to do what's suggested, feel free to return later to any or all of those activities, or to ignore them. It's *your* journey.

If you read this on your own, take it at your own pace and in any order. If you use this book in a group setting, I suggest that you read a little bit each day (in order) with the aim of completing a section each week. In the Appendix, I designed the six weekly group sessions with an introduction and ideas to spur discussion of each major division of the book. (A guide for facilitators is available as a free download from the publisher's website at www.judsonpress.com.)

Most importantly, through the act of using it, this book becomes as much yours as mine. Each of our grief journeys is unique. God bless you on your way!

PART ONE

An Invitation

Invitation to Emmaus

As a pastor, I have officiated at countless funerals. I have walked with many people as they experienced deep losses. As a human being, I have suffered my own losses: favorite pets, many relatives and acquaintances, my father. All of them impacted me, especially the death of my father. But when I lost my husband to lung cancer, my experience with grief took on a new depth of meaning. This was a new road, one with many twists and turns that I did not expect nor could I have predicted. Ed and I were soul mates; our marriage was "made in heaven," so to speak. We shared everything: the call to ministry, the love of fly-fishing, our dogs, and our extended family. I had invested everything in that relationship, so his death changed the shape of my life. I was still called to ministry. I still had my dogs and fly-fishing. Ed's children and grandchildren remained close. But he was gone, and that changed everything.

My friend Mary, then a hospice chaplain, commented that I was approaching my grief more intentionally than most people. I've often reflected on that statement. I don't know if I'm different from other people, but I do know this: I decided a long time ago that I am not going to grow into a bitter old woman. Does that sound strange? There was a point in time a number of years ago, when it seemed as if I was surrounded by bitter, angry old people. It was not a pretty sight. I didn't want to grow old that way. I figured that the only way to keep from becoming embittered was to deal with my losses as they came. To embrace God's healing for every hurt. To allow the difficulties of life to soften my heart instead of make it hard and cold. So, when Ed died, I made the only decision that made sense to me: I intentionally embraced my grief and began to seek God's healing. That decision has borne some wonderful (and surprising) fruit. Along the way, my therapist, Ruth, told me that she believed that people who embrace their grief experience transformation. She's right. And of course, the nature of transformation is such that, going into the process, you have no idea how the end of the story is going to come out. But it is a fascinating and wonderful thing. This is the transformation that happens on the road to Emmaus.

Loss is inevitable, as are the feelings associated with grief. The decision to take the road to Emmaus, however, is a choice. No doubt, because you are reading this book, you have experienced loss. I invite you to embrace your grief, make it an intentional decision, knowing that along the way, God's healing will come, perhaps in surprising ways. So come along with me on the road to Emmaus.

MY TRAVEL JOURNAL

1. What has brought you to this book?
2. Are you ready to embark on a journey? Why or why not?

SUGGESTED ITINERARY

List any obstacles that loom in your way.

Talk to God about those obstacles.

The Emmaus Story in Scripture
Luke 24:13-35

Now on that same day two of them were going to a village called
Emmaus, about seven miles from Jerusalem, and talking with
each other about all these things that had happened. While they
were talking and discussing, Jesus himself came near and went
with them, but their eyes were kept from recognizing him. And
he said to them, "What are you discussing with each other while
you walk along?" They stood still, looking sad. Then one of
them, whose name was Cleopas, answered him, "Are you the
only stranger in Jerusalem who does not know the things that
have taken place there in these days?" He asked them, "What
things?" They replied, "The things about Jesus of Nazareth, who
was a prophet mighty in deed and word before God and all the
people, and how our chief priests and leaders handed him over
to be condemned to death and crucified him. But we had hoped
that he was the one to redeem Israel. Yes, and besides all this, it
is now the third day since these things took place. Moreover,
some women of our group astounded us. They were at the tomb
early this morning, and when they did not find his body there,
they came back and told us that they had indeed seen a vision of
angels who said that he was alive. Some of those who were with
us went to the tomb and found it just as the women had said; but
they did not see him." Then he said to them, "Oh how foolish
you are, and how slow of heart to believe all that the prophets
have declared! Was it not necessary that the Messiah should suffer these things and then enter into his glory? Then beginning
with Moses and all the prophets, he interpreted to them the
things about himself in all the scriptures.

As they came near the village to which they were going, he
walked ahead as if he were going on. But they urged him strongly,
saying, "Stay with us, because it is almost evening and the day is

now nearly over." So he went in to stay with them. When he was at the table with them, he took bread, blessed and broke it, and gave it to them. Then their eyes were opened and they recognized him; and he vanished from their sight. They said to each other, "Were not our hearts burning within us while he was opening the scriptures to us?" That same hour they got up and returned to Jerusalem; and they found the eleven and their companions gathered together. They were saying, "The Lord has risen indeed, and he has appeared to Simon!" Then they told what had happened on the road, and how he had been made known to them in the breaking of the bread.

MY TRAVEL JOURNAL

1. Have you read this story before? What meaning do you glean from it?
2. What are some of the feelings experienced by the characters in the story? Can you relate to those feelings?

SUGGESTED ITINERARY

Plant a flower—contemplate the process of going from seed to bloom.

If you haven't read your Bible lately, dust it off and read an old favorite passage.

The Emmaus Story and Ours

Any time you read a familiar Bible story, you have an advantage over the characters. You've heard the story before, and you know how it will end. It's like a favorite novel or movie that you enjoy over and over again. No matter how many times you watch *It's a Wonderful Life*, for instance, George Bailey will continue to make the same mistakes. He will come to that same point of desperation every single time. And he won't "get it" until the very end. *Every time!*

This is also true for the Bible story at the heart of this book. If you've read the story before, you already know what's going to happen on the road to Emmaus, but try to keep in mind that the characters in the story are clueless. Like us, they are living their lives in a straight line, one day after the next. Events, as they come flying at them, don't always make sense. I say that in order to give you hope in your *own* dilemmas and struggles. God knows where your story is leading, and if you pay attention to God's interventions, those dilemmas and struggles can be transformed by grace, as happened in this story (Luke 24).

The story begins in Jerusalem on Easter morning. Jesus has risen from the dead, but the disciples have not yet understood that. A few of them, especially the women, have *begun* to grasp the truth, but most of them are still confused, angry, and deeply hurt. Jesus' death has devastated them. Many of the disciples have chosen to remain in Jerusalem, trying to piece their lives back together, but two of them break away and begin the long journey home. Why not? There's nothing more they can do for Jesus. He's gone.

You know the feeling. The funeral is over; the food is gone; and people are talked out. It's time to try and get back to some sort of normalcy.

As Cleopas and his companion walk on the long road to Emmaus, hot and downcast, a stranger joins them. Amazingly, this stranger seems to be ignorant about what has taken place in Jerusalem over the past several days. His ignorance astounds them. Everybody in Jerusalem knows what happened to Jesus! It has been in all the tabloids.

The stranger *is* Jesus, and of course he knows what has happened. But Jesus feigns ignorance in order to help them at this critical turning point. Telling their story is important for them. As the two forlorn disciples recount their story, they reveal a great deal about themselves: where they are emotionally and where they are in their beliefs. They make some very strong statements about Jesus and what he has done, and then they reveal their hearts: "but we had hoped." *We had hoped that he was the one to redeem Israel* (or *we had hoped that he was the one to set Israel free*).

Like so many others, they saw Jesus as the Messiah, *and* they believed that it was the Messiah's job to set Israel free from the Roman government. Jesus had let them down. He let himself get killed instead. *We had hoped*, they said. *We had hoped.* But their hopes are decimated now. It's over.

For them, the crucifixion was a failure. Not only a failure for Jesus and his ministry, but also for his followers, who had invested everything in him, and who now looked like a bunch of idiots for having done so. But often something that looks like failure is really an opportunity to find a new and better direction. Thomas Edison, for instance, was tossed out of elementary school when his teachers decided he couldn't do the work. So he tried inventing things, and he did rather well ("I have had a lot of success with failure," he once said). Harry S. Truman tried to be a haberdasher and failed miserably. So he tried politics.

The disciples had placed a great deal of faith and hope in Jesus. They *believed* in him. Still, their faith and hope were aimed in the wrong direction because what they believed was wrong. It was as big a fantasy as Sidd Finch. Do you know about Sidd Finch? On April 1, 1985, *Sports Illustrated* ran one of its most celebrated articles, "The Curious Case of Sidd Finch," a lengthy feature about a rising star Mets pitcher who could fire a baseball at the amazing speed of 168 miles an hour. It made for wonderful reading, but much like the famous Orson Welles radio play *War of the Worlds,* it was fiction. An April Fool's joke. An effective one, too, because more than twenty years later, people still approach Joe Burton, who was the man in the photographs, and recognize him as Sidd Finch.

The idea of Jesus as Messiah, however, was no April Fool's joke. It was a genuine hope and dream. Jesus *was* the Messiah, but his followers greatly misunderstood. Right up until the crucifixion, the disciples were trying to make him into their fantasy Messiah. The liberator of Israel. A conquering king. It is in this moment on the Emmaus road that these false hopes are revealed for what they truly are. False. *"We had hoped that he was the one to redeem Israel."* We had hoped. But we hope no more. It's over.

When people make up fantasies like the *War of the Worlds* and "The Curious Case of Sidd Finch," they are trying to create something bigger than life. When you're dealing with God, though, you discover that very often the truth is more remarkable, more powerful, and harder to believe than any fiction. And that is one of the things that emerges on the road to Emmaus. But the journey doesn't begin there. It begins with letting go of the fantasy—what you thought was going to be, but isn't.

"But we had hoped." This is a phrase that haunts me, and it is the phrase that has led me to write this book. I am convinced that the road to healing begins in this place of letting go.

Some time after Ed died, I started walking the Emmaus road. My journey to Emmaus started not with his death, but with a *thought* about his death. One day it came to me: *marriage is not forever.* Now, that may not sound like a very profound thought, but it was to me. When I married Ed, I thought it was forever. That was because I knew without a doubt that God had brought Ed into my life. It was exceedingly clear. So, I thought that the shape of my life was an identity forever merged with his. My future would always include him. We had thoughts and plans about how that future would look.

Then he was gone, and I was headed for Emmaus. *You see, we had hoped . . .*

The road to Emmaus often begins in a fog of confusion. When the fog clears, it becomes obvious that you are on a new road. You have left the past behind, yet it's not clear what the future will be. In a very real sense, this is a walk of faith.

It's not easy to begin, because the road looks bleak at the start. The landscape may be dull and gray, or perhaps hazardous like driving on a steep mountain road with no guard rails. It's a long way down, and the one thing that's sure is that you are on this road alone. You may have some companions and supporters, but the road is yours to walk, or run, or drive. Or not.

Just tonight I spoke to a young woman who is moving to another state with her husband and young son. She's lived here all her life, yet she knows in her heart that this move is the right thing to do. It terrifies her all the same. It feels like stepping off a cliff because so much is unknown. It may seem strange to compare the grief journey to such a move, because you may not feel that grief is a choice. After all, you didn't ask for this. It was thrust upon you by the death of someone you love. Yet it *is* a choice. Emmaus is out there to be discovered and experienced. Some will find it. Others will not.

The first sure sign that you have started the journey to Emmaus is that deep, startling awareness that the road you were on has suddenly come to a dead end.

Think about your own unfulfilled fantasies. How would you finish the phrase: "We had hoped . . ."? What have you hoped for that has not happened? What plans have been thwarted? What things have you thought were God's will, yet they have not been accomplished? What has been lost because one you have loved has died?

Walk with me to Emmaus. It's a tough road, but there is a miracle waiting at the end. I don't want to take you there too quickly, though, or the road to recovery might simply be perceived as a quick fix, which it is not. For now, I ask you to trust the God who raised Jesus from the dead. God raised Jesus from the dead, but God did not prevent Jesus from dying. Nor did God prevent the disciples from deep grief. God will not keep your loved ones from dying, nor you from grief. But God will be with you every step along the way, and because of that profound truth, the Emmaus miracle can be yours as well.

MY TRAVEL JOURNAL

1. Finish the phrase *"But we had hoped. . . ."* What dreams have been lost because your loved one is gone?

2. What do you need from God today? Talk to God about that.

SUGGESTED ITINERARY

Take a walk. Take note of what you see, hear, and smell.

Make the first entry in your journal.

Hard Reality

It was a late August day; the feel of autumn was in the air. At eleven o'clock, I visited a woman whom I had been counseling for several weeks. Her home had been stripped nearly bare as she readied herself for a move out of state. The only furniture visible was a card table with two lonely-looking chairs in the kitchen. Her marriage was ending, and she was preparing to begin a new life in a new environment. It was a bittersweet meeting because she felt a lot of support and encouragement and direction from God and from our conversations, yet she felt great loss because the years of her husband's infidelity weighed on her mind and heart. She had tears in her eyes as I left her because it was, more than likely, to be our last meeting before her move.

I couldn't linger, because I had a lunch appointment with my friend Brenda. Our lunches had become much less frequent in the past months because her physical concerns had become very burdensome. Often she simply couldn't get out. Today she was in great turmoil because her only son was about to become a father faraway in Texas, and she was not at all sure that she would be physically able to go to be supportive of the new parents and to see her new grandchild.

Feeling a bit weighed down by other people's troubles, I stopped briefly at home after lunch to share the leftovers of my sandwich with my Labradors, Grace and Misty, before returning to the office. Before I went in the house, I checked the hummingbird feeder. For the last couple of days a praying mantis had been visiting the feeder, grabbing, I presumed, a snack of ants and other bugs. Every fall I look forward to the return of these insect giants. I had taken some time trying to get good photographs on her earlier visits to the hummingbird feeder, and I was curious whether she might have returned. Indeed she had, but it was not a happy return, at least not for me. It was for the mantis, though. The insect was happily ensconced on the hummingbird feeder, hanging upside down and *eating a hummingbird*! That was too much. Now *I* wanted to cry! The hummingbirds were my pride and joy. Now I felt as though, unwittingly, I had been an accomplice in the death of a friend. Later, upon close examination, my husband discovered that the tiny bird that had since been discarded by the mantis was whole—on the outside. Its insides had been vacuumed out by the green monster. I hadn't the heart to take part in the post mortem. A couple of days later, when I could stomach the search, I found a site on the Internet that confirmed my suspicion that this was not a once-in-a-lifetime event. Praying mantises love to eat hummingbirds, along with tree frogs, lizards, and mice. Still, it didn't seem right. It took me a long time to get over it. Perhaps I'm not over it yet.

So many things in life seem so unfair: the infidelity of one's spouse; unexplainable, unfixable medical conditions; even death itself. Unfair, perhaps, but very very real. It may be possible for a while, perhaps even for a long enjoyable season, to sustain the illusion that the world is perfectly ordered to our specifications—but for all of us, sooner or later, something comes along to burst that bubble.

Reality is tough to deal with. But in the long run, it is easier, and certainly healthier, to live in the real world than in a fantasy world where everything is supposed to turn out the way I want it to. Think about it. In a fantasy world, you have to work hard to first create and then sustain those illusions in the face of a stubborn reality that presents its own truth. Reality is more painful to be sure, but the real world is where healing is possible. It's the people who deal with reality (instead of living in denial or avoidance) who are most able to achieve a measure of peace and wholeness.

During difficult times, many people quote the familiar serenity prayer. But did you know that there is more to the prayer than the six lines that most people have memorized? Perhaps now is a good time to reflect on the entire prayer and its meaning for your journey to Emmaus:

God grant me the serenity
to accept the things
    I cannot change,
Courage to change the things
    I can, and the wisdom
    to know the difference.

Living one day at a time;
Enjoying one moment at a time;
    Accepting hardship as the
    pathway to peace.

N.b.

Taking, as He did, this sinful world
as it is, not as I would have it;

Trusting that He will make all things
right if I surrender to His will;

That I may be reasonably happy
    in this life,
And supremely happy with Him
    forever in the next.[1]

MY TRAVEL JOURNAL

1. What are some of the hard realities that you have seen recently?

2. Are you ready to accept these as true (even though you don't like them)?

SUGGESTED ITINERARY

Take a few minutes to reflect on the Serenity Prayer. What do you want to say to God today? Go ahead—God is listening.

Make a collage of pictures. Take note of your feelings as you do so.

Note

1. Reinhold Niebuhr is credited with writing at least the first six lines of this prayer. Others may have contributed the remainder.

The Journey before the Journey

On the road to Emmaus, the two disciples were "talking with each other about all these things that had happened." Not only talking about the death of Jesus, I suspect, but also his life and their shared hopes. These two had spent much time with Jesus. They had come to love him, trust him, respect him. They had many shared experiences to recall, in addition to the experience of his death. Those experiences were reflected in the sadness of their faces that day. And it was those experiences that made the walk to Emmaus necessary. I can imagine them sharing all the "what ifs" as well as the "remember whens."

No one's grief begins in a vacuum. The journey of grief presupposes a relationship; there is a story behind those tears. Many stories, I suppose. The fact that you are grieving now means that you have spent quality time with your loved one. You talked, bonded, and dreamed. You struggled together, failed together, succeeded together. Much relational water has gone over the dam.

Grief comes from a relationship. Even Jesus grieved, as you may remember. The Gospel of John tells a poignant story about the death of Lazarus. This is a rare intimate look at Jesus and his friends, the sibling trio of Mary, Martha, and Lazarus. It is important to notice in this story that Jesus has the power to heal Lazarus *before* he dies, and he has the power to give Lazarus his life back *after* he has died. Jesus knows all that. Yet, when he stands outside the tomb where Lazarus has been laid, Jesus weeps. His tears are not missed by the others who are by the tomb. "See how he loved him!" they say (John 11:36). And that's what grief is about. It's about loving someone and losing that someone you have loved. If even Jesus grieved—he who had the power to give Lazarus back his life—then certainly we can be allowed to grieve, too. It's not a sign of weakness to cry. It's a sign of love.

I'll never forget the day I met Ed, or rather, when I first saw him across the room. It was in church, of course. I had just taken on a new pastorate in Fircrest, Washington. It was a small congregation worshiping in a multipurpose room. Just four or five rows of folding chairs filled the space to capacity. When I stepped up to the pulpit, I noticed a man in the back row whom I had not met before. He was dressed in Western garb, from the leather jacket to his boots, to the Stetson stowed under his chair. What I didn't know until much later was that two of my most aggressive greeters had sweetly plopped him down between them and said, "You're just going to love our new little woman pastor."

I had never given much thought to love at first sight, perhaps because it had never happened. But I have to admit there was an instant attraction. The problem was that he escaped out the door before I could talk to him. Not just that Sunday, but several Sundays in a row. I was intrigued, because it took a real escape artist to slip out of that small building without talking to me!

Then one day he showed up at my office door. My secretary reached into a file drawer and pulled out Ed's welcome letter that had come back because he had given us the wrong address. When I came to the door, his first words to me were, "I think we have a problem." It turned out that the problem had to do with his mother. She had been widowed for a number of years and was about to remarry. The wedding was scheduled to be on Monday (which he noted was my day off), and they needed a preacher. He didn't know if I would agree to perform a wedding on my day off. Hence the problem. Well, that relieved my mind, at least for a while. At least *I* wasn't the problem. Not yet, anyway! His next line was a classic: "If you marry my mother, I'll eventually join your church." Well, I was new in the ministry, but I had already heard similar lines more than a few times. I was still intrigued by this rather handsome cowboy, though, so I agreed to do the wedding. What amazed me was that he intended to keep his promise. He kept coming back, and one day he said, "I'm ready to join the church." I told him that he would have to take a class first. He balked, saying that even though he was raised a Baptist, he knew all about being a Presbyterian because he went to Lewis and Clark College (a Presbyterian school). We fenced about that for a bit, and he finally asked me to lunch (he claimed *I* was the one who issued the invitation) across the Tacoma Narrows Bridge in Gig Harbor where he was running a laundry and dry cleaning establishment. We could continue the conversation there. After lunch we walked down the main street and stopped in at a kitchen shop where he bought me a gift. It was a thin green rubber disk about the size of a CD—a jar opener! It may not sound romantic to you, but I treasured that gift for years, until it literally fell apart.

The rest, as they say, is history. We were on our second date at a place called the Cellar, eating steamed clams, when he asked me to marry him. I wanted to say yes, but it felt *way* too soon. So I asked for time. While he waited, I mulled over our differences and wondered if it could work. I was doing a mental checklist of the potential issues and problems one day while we were in his car on our way back from dinner. His divorce and financial problems topped the list. Our thirteen-year age difference also figured in. He was a smoker, which I didn't like. And he drank too much, it seemed to me. He was estranged from his daughters, and that didn't feel right. Yet there was something genuine about him, something that seemed to portend a good future. Could this be right for me? There came what was (to me at least) a barely audible voice that I recognized as coming from God: "Could *my* choice be a wrong choice?" Well, no, I guess not. Eventually, I said yes.

The next twenty-two years were filled with stories that include his going to seminary and entering the ministry. Our serving churches together in Alaska, California, Oregon, and New Jersey. His reunion with his daughters, Kim and Tami, their eventual marriages, and our grandchildren, Caleb (aka Sparky) and Sarah (aka Princess). Our dog family, starting with his black Lab, Rowdy, then Buck, Ramey, Spike, Misty, and Grace. Fishing trips to the Metolius River, the Mad River, and the Delaware River. Trips to see family, for weddings and funerals. Friends.

The first year of marriage was the hardest—each of us adjusting to the other's preferences and foibles. And there were tough times, especially as we tried to understand ministry in conflicted churches, while battling our own personal demons as well. But as the years went by and we both grew and developed, we reached a point of understanding and acceptance as well as love. There were no secrets between us and no serious unfinished business. Except that I really wish that he had written that book about anger and domestic violence that only he could write. Instead, he was too busy counseling people, helping them to reshape their lives and relationships. So busy he hardly had time to die. But die he did, and that began my new journey. My grief journey has been shaped by all that we shared, all of our struggles, all that we learned together, and all that we still hoped to do.

I am now a solo pastor. I don't mind that; it's how I started out in ministry. But I miss his partnership, especially his gift for counseling people in situations of domestic violence and his eagerness to work with emergency situations. I have had to adjust my priorities in ministry. I have had to learn how to barbecue. And dust. And I've had to surrender to a new view of the future.

One Death, Many Griefs

Sometimes the road to Emmaus gets a little congested. What has been profoundly obvious to me is that, even though I was Ed's most intimate relationship, I am not the only one who grieved his passing. Everyone whose life he touched has had their own grief. One death, but many griefs, and each one is different because the relationship was different. To some, Ed was a father figure or a mentor. His counseling touched many, and some who knew him in that relationship grieved long and hard. So did those who knew him as a pastor.

So did his daughters, but for them the road to Emmaus has been pretty rocky. In order to explain their experience, I need to tell you a thumbnail story of Ed's life before he and I met. He sometimes spoke of his "checkered past." When I met him, he was just emerging from that past. But I really only knew him on the plus side of the ledger. Here's the other side. When Ed was in high school in the Dalles, Oregon, he had thoughts of going into the ministry. His parents were dead set against it. Not that they had anything against the ministry; they just didn't want their son in a profession that they felt would provide an inadequate living. He did not have the assertiveness at the time to buck their attitude, so he went off to college in nearby Portland, graduated, and went off to make his fortune (something he wasn't very good at). He married Babs when he was working for Boeing in New Orleans. Soon after, they moved back to Portland and started their family. They had two daughters, Kim and Tami. When their marriage fell apart, Kim was six and Tami was three. The divorce was messy and bitter, and the children were caught in the middle. Eventually, Babs moved the kids out of state, and Ed stopped paying child support. For many years he did not see them, and though, as he told me later, he desperately longed for them, he was afraid to try and make contact. His only outreach to them was through token cards and small gifts for Christmas and birthdays.

Immediately after the divorce, he married a woman named Wanda, and that started ten years of downward spiraling—financially, emotionally, and spiritually. Besides his failure to be a good husband and father, he had also become embroiled in dishonest business practices. At the time, he was a traveling salesman, moving from town to town in a fifth-wheel trailer, trying to resurrect a failing business. His only friend in the world was his black Lab, Rowdy. Finally, Ed came to a point of no return. He hated the person he had become and made plans to commit suicide. He was driving in his pickup truck with his gun in his lap, looking for a secluded place. It was dark and rainy. Suddenly a soft light enveloped him. Now, remember, he was not a very spiritual person at this point. He was not looking for God, but God was looking for him.

The story he told me about this event goes something like this: Ed cried out to God with a phrase he did not recognize at the time, but would later discover in the Bible: "My God, my God, why have you forsaken me?"

He heard a voice: "I haven't forsaken you. You've forsaken me."
"What do I have to do?"
"Follow me."

That was his turning point. He gave his life back to God and immediately got in touch with his brother Bill, who was in a position to help him financially and emotionally. Bill lived in Tacoma, Washington, which coincidentally is next door to Fircrest, where I had just started my new pastoral position.

After Ed and I were married for about a year, he felt a renewal of his call to the ministry, and with some struggle, he said "yes" and started seminary. He also reconnected with his daughters who were, by then, teenagers.

I'd like to say that his relationship with his daughters was fully repaired, but it wasn't. There was a reconnection, and we enjoyed many get-togethers with them, but there was always a barrier that could not be crossed. A wound that would not heal.

My biggest regret is that other people got the good side of Ed: the counselor, the father figure, the compassionate friend. His daughters never fully experienced his transformation. Their memory, still, is of a man who was unfaithful both as a father to them and as a husband to their mother—a person who should have nurtured them in their growing years, but instead brought them great pain. That reality has figured big in their grief. I will let them share their own perspectives.

TAMI: *I still miss him, and I still miss the relationship we could have had if circumstances had been different. I regret that we didn't really bond the way a father and daughter should. . . . Dad was always in the back of my mind as some mysterious force growing up. I remember at one point when I was a child, having a dream where I was following a man in the mall. He had a beard and was with a woman. I followed him for quite a while, nervous and scared, but excited. Finally, I tapped him and told him he was my father. He said, "I know," and turned his back on me. I guess those feelings of abandonment were stronger than I liked to realize or admit.*

I was angry with him for leaving us.

I was angry with him for making Mom tell us he was leaving, and not doing his dirty work himself.

I was angry with him for the way he treated Mom.

I was angry with him for lying.

I was angry with him for not showing any interest in us.

I was angry with him for cutting us out of his family.

I was angry with him for his "adopted daughter."

I was angry with him for being able to help others while he was unwilling to help us.

I was angry with him for leaving just as I started to feel like I was getting to know him. He was always leaving. Leaving, moving away, now dying.

I still get angry.

However, like I tell Paul, while Dad wasn't able to be a father, he was obviously able to be a good counselor. He helped a lot of people, and I think he was only able to do that because he had been so deep in the pit himself. You have to know pain to heal it, and at the funeral it became obvious through all the stories people told that Dad was able to use his own faults and mistakes to help others deal with their own.

KIM: *While I miss and loved my Dad, my grieving is mostly for what never was, and what never will be.*

I can't say that my Dad and I ever formed a good relationship. He was a person I knew who was eventually special to me because he was my father, but I was never comfortable with him and I never trusted him. I believe he tried, but too much had happened between us. There was too much hurt and anger on my part. Obviously, he still sometimes would say or do something that would hurt me, and I don't know that he ever fully realized the damage he had done. I think he had told himself so many lies to try and excuse what he had done, that at times he actually believed he hadn't done anything wrong.

There isn't a day that goes by that I don't think about him; sometimes I remember the good things, but a lot of times I think about all the destruction and hurt. Even though I've forgiven, I can't forget, nor could I trust him not to hurt me again, and I think that's why we could never cross those barriers. I have to take some responsibility for that. I have to make a conscious effort to forgive over and over and think about the good that happened after we reconciled and about all the good he did for others. He did form a relationship with my children, and that was important to all of us. I have some wonderful memories and pictures of them together as well as some great vacations for all of us, but there was always an awkwardness between us that stood in the way of bringing us truly together.

At the funeral, after hearing the testimonies of others as to the help and counseling he gave to so many others, I broke down crying. I remember when my Uncle Bill spoke at the funeral, he said that the person everyone was talking about was not the person we knew, and he was right. It was so hard for me to reconcile what I was hearing with what I knew and had experienced. It broke my heart to know that all these people received from him what should have been mine.

Part of my healing process is knowing that everything that happened in my dad's life and how his decisions affected my life were all part of God's plans. I don't think he would have been as effective as a minister and counselor if he hadn't gone through what he went through. He could relate to these people because he had been there. I also wouldn't be the person I am if these things hadn't happened to me. God had it planned, and that helps me accept it and it helps with the forgiveness. I don't know why God took him away again, especially since he finally seemed to have his act together and was helping so many. I'll never understand God's plans, but I don't think I have to—I just have to accept it and know that good came from all the bad, and that's how I am healing. I know I'll have scars forever, but those scars make me who I am today just as Dad's scars made him who he was.

When I read what Kim and Tami have written, it seems as if they are writing about a different person than I am writing about. And indeed they are. Ed became a very different person in his later years, but neither he nor his daughters could undo that painful past. The scars remain. Both Kim and Tami have much more to say about their *journey before the journey* and how that has affected their walk to Emmaus. But I trust that these comments give you a glimpse into their struggle. I also hope that they give you encouragement. For instance, it's okay to be angry; it's okay to struggle with forgiveness; and it's okay to be honest with yourself about the dark side of the person you have lost.

Before you get too far in your walk to Emmaus, I suggest that you take stock of the journey *before* the journey. Tell your story, write it, and picture it. Do whatever will help you to understand the nature of that relationship and what may still need to be resolved. One powerful thing that I did, in connection with taking Ed's ashes to be scattered in Oregon, was to put together a combination video/picture presentation, with a music background. It showed pictures of him as a child, with his brother and other family members, his first wife and daughters, the grandkids, our life in ministry, our dogs, and some fishing video clips. The process of creating that presentation was profoundly therapeutic for me, and it was a way to share with others the depth of our relationship. It's only twelve minutes long, but it has the potential to elicit powerful memories every time I look at it. I play the DVD on special days when I want to just remember, and cry.

Like Kim and Tami, you may well have some tough memories to heal. It's all a part of the journey. Keep in mind that you are not traveling to Fantasy Island. It's the road to Emmaus, which is to say it's about reality. If the relationship with the person who died was difficult, you may well find *more* difficulty in your grief instead of less. But the healing principle remains the same. Embrace your grief. Deal with your feelings. *Let* God heal your heart. It will take time, perhaps more time than you thought.

MY TRAVEL JOURNAL

1. What was unique about your loved one? What are some special moments that you shared? What will always be in your heart because of this person?

2. How has your relationship with your loved one influenced the nature and the duration of your grief?

SUGGESTED ITINERARY

Try telling the story of your relationship to someone.

Make a photo or video collage. Chronicle the relationship in a way that is meaningful for you.

Find an old picture that shows both you and your loved one. If it's not already framed, find a frame that fits the occasion represented by the picture.

Margie's Story

Chaotic is the word that Margie uses to describe her life with Hank. "He spun an orbit of chaos and took me with him." From an outsider's viewpoint, the relationship was stormy at best. It was the classic emotional roller coaster; she felt great love for her husband yet felt controlled by his abusive behavior. Hank was both handsome and charming, and he adored his kids, but he was very high maintenance as a spouse. Margie describes Hank as heartbroken; someone who bounced between self-loathing and narcissism. His attitude toward himself often emerged as tension in the marriage. Margie was in and out of counseling about the relationship and had contemplated divorce on more than one occasion. Their age difference (he was seven years younger than Margie) added to the stress.

Margie describes Hank as someone who "pushed the envelope." He was very active, loved to play, and tended toward recklessness in his sports. He asked Margie and the kids to join him for a weekend of motocross racing, the sport that had most recently captured his attention. The kids went, but Margie (weary of the relationship issues with Hank) stayed home. Before he left, he told Margie, "I'm gonna ride with absolutely no fear." In the race, he made a poorly executed jump and was killed on impact.

Hank died on September 26, 2004. He was thirty-five and Margie was forty-two. In addition to Margie, Hank left two young children: Hank Jr. was nine and a half, and Kelly was seven. Margie's older daughter, Amanda, who considered Hank her father, was twenty.

When Hank died, Margie immediately went into shock. At the same time she felt remorse about a prayer she had prayed just a couple of weeks earlier. "I can't take it anymore," she had cried to God. When Hank died, she felt guilty about that prayer, as if the prayer had caused his accident. She knew in her heart that it wasn't her fault, but the guilt remained.

Some people who observed Margie's experience expected her to move through grief quickly because, after all, she and Hank had such a rocky marriage. "She's better off without him," was the general attitude. "She'll quickly move on." The opposite has been the case.

She did move on quickly in a couple of respects, though. Hank had been working in a construction business with his brothers and had also begun some home improvement projects. When he died, he left behind numerous unfinished projects and a few promised but not begun. Margie immediately began to remodel her home and made it a place that more reflected her personality and tastes. And she began dating. The dating has met some needs but overall has not been satisfying, and thus far has not led to a lasting relationship. "I have extremely bad luck with men," Margie said to me recently.

From the beginning, Margie's grief has been a tough and arduous journey. It took four days for the funeral home to arrange to bring Hank's body back to New Jersey from New York, where he had the accident. Those four days were excruciating as she waited for the chance to find a measure of reality in a very surrealistic time. On the day of Hank's funeral, the family had the opportunity for a private visitation before the public viewing. Hank Jr. would not go in at first. Margie went in with Kelly's hand in hers. She looked down at her young daughter, saw the tears in Kelly's eyes, and thought immediately, "I want to kill him."

In the early months of her grief, Margie kept her social contacts somewhat at arm's length, including her church friends. People were very caring and wanted to know how she was doing. She didn't want to tell them, because she was still too raw, too full of emotion. Could they handle it? She wasn't sure. So she stayed away. Then, gradually, as she felt stronger, she started filtering back into her normal activities. At her church, Margie is known as one who is always thinking of projects to reach out to other people, especially to kids and to women who are in abusive relationships. She has been an integral member of the church's music ministry. For a time she stepped away from all of that, but gradually she has been returning to those ministries. She has also begun to find a new focus for ministry. Margie is a language whiz and recently finished her bachelor's degree with a major in Spanish and a minor in French. She has a great desire to help people from other cultures find their way in our American society. As a first step, she has begun helping to translate for bilingual couples in premarital counseling.

"I was in a daze for two years," Margie says of her grief journey. Now it's been three years, and her primary emotion today is anger. Guilt comes a close second. She feels guilty for not being with Hank when he died, and guilty for her anger toward him. Yet her anger has been empowering. Not long ago, she got a letter from the township telling her she needed to clean up her yard. Hank was a collector, and the yard was littered with his junk. "Could they not have sent that letter when Hank was alive?" Margie fumed. At first she cried over the overwhelming task. Then she was sad. And then angry. She started tearing things apart and throwing them into Hank's truck. With every trip to the dump she felt stronger. "I can do whatever I have to do," she said.

The challenges continue to come. Her brother recently died from liver failure after years of alcohol abuse. Her daughter Amanda came within inches of losing her life in a car accident. Margie describes her reactions to these events as a kind of post-traumatic shock syndrome. Each new trauma that comes is jarring, as she relives the pain and shock that came when Hank died. The sense of chaos returns for a time as she again has to reconfigure her life.

At the three-year point in her grief, Emmaus still seems far in the distance, but she has also found a measure of peace. Her home life was once marked by chaos but is now ordered and peaceful ("Now *I* make the decisions," she says). She has also found solace in God in the midst of her deep wounds. "It's almost like Hank's death has helped me to get to where I need to be spiritually, which is to let go of the things of this world." When she was younger, her goal was to have a nice life: a nice companion and nice things. Now, she says, "When I wake up in the morning, what I want is to live the kind of life that's pleasing to God."

MY TRAVEL JOURNAL

1. What part of Margie's story do you relate to?

2. If you were Margie's friend, what would you do to help her with her grief?

SUGGESTED ITINERARY

Write a note of encouragement to someone who can use it, or write a thank-you to someone who has encouraged you.

PART TWO

Preparations

Packing Your Bags

From the first summer of our marriage, Ed and I took an annual fishing trip. Over the years, we developed a simple routine for getting ready. It was easy to decide what to take: fishing gear, casual clothes, rain gear, food, dogs. As the years went by, we got the packing down to a science. I knew how to arrange things so that everything would fit. The preparations took some work, but they were simple nonetheless. I knew what to expect.

Other kinds of trips are not as easy to prepare for as our annual fishing trip was. There are a lot of unknowns. Where will I stay? Do I need dress-up clothes? An extra jacket? A dog sitter?

The road to Emmaus is more like the second kind of journey. I don't entirely know what to expect, so how do I pack? What do I do to prepare? *Can* I prepare? Some might even ask, *should* I prepare? Isn't preparing for grief a kind of giving in, a fatalistic acceptance of the inevitable? Shouldn't I fight for the lives of those I love, instead of morosely preparing for their demise?

Maybe I should call it grief *training* instead of preparation. Loss is a part of life, and there is much to be learned from each event. It's possible, I believe, to train one's "grieving muscles" in the smaller losses, so as to be more in shape for the marathon walk to Emmaus. Even if you are well on the way to Emmaus, it's not too late for training. If you look back, you may even discover that in previous losses, you have already received significant grief training.

The key to grief training is listening. Listen to the experiences of other people, and listen to yourself. Let yourself grow through these experiences.

Though I've never been one to enjoy travelogues or to enjoy watching other people's home videos, I open my ears when people talk about their life experiences. Especially their road to Emmaus experiences.

There are four people whose experiences have greatly shaped my own perspectives and experience of grief: two elderly gentlemen—Ed and Larry—were great models for me. When Ed's wife, Virginia, was diagnosed with Lou Gehrig's disease, it was devastating to both of them. But Virginia was a fighter, and Ed was a problem solver. So while Virginia did all she could to battle her disease, Ed took care of the practical aspects of things, like setting up a phone system that she would be able to use even after her vocal strength was gone. As medical bills mounted, he made plans to get Virginia the care she needed, even to the point of considering a move to an "old soldiers' home" so that she could benefit from the sale of the house (it never came to that). He was always thinking, always taking each new challenge by the horns. And then Virginia died. Ed tackled his grief the same way he took on any other challenge, this time taking care of himself—riding his bicycle, working on his computer, helping out at church.

It was the same with Larry, who lost his wife, Audrey, to Alzheimer's. Each step of the way, Larry dealt with the information as it came and made the best decisions possible for Audrey's care, first at home and then at a local nursing home when home care became untenable. In the aftermath of her death, he continued to deal with life as it came, grieving deeply, yet living his life as well.

What I so admire about both of these men is hard to put into words. Practical? Yes. Productive? Indeed. Good problem solvers, both of them. Realistic to the core. And deeply feeling. Audrey has been gone for several years now, and Larry just recently died. It was just a few weeks before he died that he was talking to me about Audrey. "I still miss her," Larry said to me. I want to be able to have that kind of caring, giving attitude and that same ability to think realistically about my life.

Two other people have impacted me significantly—my mother and her sister, my Aunt Louise.

My Aunt Louise is in her upper nineties now, and she still lives by herself. She has arthritis in her back and two artificial hips. More to the point of this discussion, she has outlived two husbands and both of her sons. Her first husband and her sons all died suddenly from heart attacks. Her second husband died from cancer. Losses enough to make one a bitter old woman. But she is not. Yes, life sometimes gets her down, but she has grieved each loss as it has come and has kept on with life. When I talk to her, I love to hear her talk about the things she thinks about—the price of corn, current events in the world. She has not withdrawn into herself, but keeps in touch with her friends, her family, her world. It's not easy, but she does it.

My mom also has outlived two husbands. Like Aunt Louise, she has arthritis and she has had both knees and both hips replaced. She is eighty-eight and is just now making plans to move into an assisted living apartment. Since my mom has never been one to share her feelings, what I mostly have to go on is her behavior. When my father died (I was eighteen, the last kid out of the house), she more or less sprang into action. It didn't seem practical at the time for her to stay on the family farm in South Dakota where we had all grown up. My dad had been able to fix pretty much everything, but at the time of his death, things were not in good repair. And Mom needed a job. At fifty-one, she was too young for Social Security, and there were no savings to fall back on. Two out of four kids were out of college and on their own, and the last two were eligible for help from Social Security. But one needs to eat! My dad died in late June, and by late August, Mom had moved into town and had a job as a teacher's aide in the local school. She rented the farm out to a neighbor for added income. Several years later, she gave up the teacher's aide job and moved to North Dakota to marry her second husband. I admire her for her willingness to take risks, to make significant moves and adjustments in order to continue on in life.

As you contemplate your own Emmaus journey, listen to the stories of others. Pay attention to the things that helped them and the things that did not. As I have watched other people deal with grief, I have begun to understand what things are most important to me. You have already figured it out: dealing with reality, embracing feelings, and living life to the fullest. It is usually easier to observe things in other people than it is to see them in yourself.

But let your heart connect with those other stories, and let your heart be your teacher.

At the same time, cultivate the ability to listen to your own journey. You have already had many losses, and you have developed some ways of coping. How are those ways working for you? Do you need to be open to some new skills and abilities?

For me, it all started with a stuffed rabbit, a story that I have told at length elsewhere.[1] I was just a small child, and that rabbit was a constant companion for me. Then it was gone, for good. I never did find out what happened to it, though I searched for it high and low. I suspected, much later, that my mom had thrown it away, but she has no memory of it. My memory is simply of the loss. The feelings that I felt then are the same as those I feel at every loss: sadness, frustration, confusion, longing. Other losses in my youth included the kittens that were born in the barn every spring (sometimes we had more than a dozen). Each was given a name and loved through the summer, but most of them died in the fall from distemper. I grieved long and hard for each one. I even grieved for the garden in the fall. When the last of the pumpkins was gathered into the cellar, I felt a great sadness that the growing season was over. The thing was that in spring, it was almost like a reincarnation. The garden started up again, and more kittens were born (and usually given the same names as the kittens the year before). The stuffed rabbit was gone for good, though, and when I turned eighteen, so was my dad. With those losses, life entered a new dimension. Nothing would be the same again.

Because my family was not good with expressing feelings, I coped with my dad's death by turning inward. I was already an introvert, so that wasn't hard. The thing that was noticeable, though, was a physical reality. Before my dad died, my feelings all went to the back of my neck. I had a wrenching pain every morning when I rode the bus to school. It gradually went away during the day but was back like clockwork the next morning. After he died, the pain went away. But on an emotional level, I was mostly numb. In retrospect, that experience made me listen more to my body. When I have a neck or back pain, I ask myself what's going on emotionally. Usually there's something. Also in retrospect, the experience made me want to learn to understand and deal with my feelings. Because my family wasn't good with feelings, I had to go elsewhere. I was just starting college, and that meant new friends, a chance to open up in new ways. That was a good start. And at each new stage of life, I have tried to open up the feeling channels more and more. What I have noticed over a process of many years is that I still have a tendency to go back to old familiar roads. The roads of not feeling, not expressing, not being vulnerable.

All of these observations and experiences have been, in some measure, preparatory to my Emmaus journey. But there were some other very specific preparations that were closer to the present.

It started with Buck. Buck was our yellow Labrador retriever who had been with us since our time in Alaska. After Buck came Ramey, a six-month-old female black Lab who quickly became the love of Buck's life. From Buck and Ramey came nine black pups, one of whom we kept. For a good many years, Ed and I enjoyed our Labrador family of Buck, Ramey, and Spike. Then Buck got an undiagnosed illness and quickly died. The illusion of permanence was quickly deflated, and I grieved hard for that dog. Ed and I grieved together, and I *felt* more grief than I had ever felt before. Another yellow Lab—Misty—was brought into the family. Then came Ed's sixtieth birthday. Ed was thirteen years older than I, but I never really felt that difference until he turned sixty and I was forty-seven. I had an uneasy feeling that sixty was the beginning of the end. There wasn't any logical reason for me to have that feeling. Ed wasn't sick, and in this day and age, sixty is still relatively young. But as it turned out, the feeling was prophetic. Two years later, he was diagnosed with lung cancer. In the meantime, we experienced several other preparatory events, mostly related to our dogs.

Shortly after 9/11, which was a watershed for us all, Spike was diagnosed with a melanoma in his left eye and had the eye removed. At the same time he was diagnosed with laryngeal paralysis and was scheduled for surgery. Then Misty tore her cruciate ligament. The two dogs had surgery the same day. A month later Ramey died. In early June that same year ('02), we got Amazing

Grace, a full-of-mischief chocolate Labrador. A week later came Ed's cancer diagnosis. Had the diagnosis come first, we may well have decided it was no time to get a puppy. But the puppy had already wormed her way into our hearts, and Amazing Grace has dogged my steps ever since. An interesting choice of names, and a wonderful reminder of God's intervention and care.

You can't prepare for everything. No doubt you have stepped onto an airplane or into a motel room and suddenly remembered what you forgot. Or found that the trip didn't turn out as you planned, and you needed things you never would have imagined. The same is true on the road to Emmaus. You can't predict everything that's going to happen, so you need to lean on God's amazing grace to provide for you. But God also provides in other ways along the way. So take the time to listen to the stories of people who have experienced loss. It will help them to tell the story, and it may help you later in ways you never could predict. And listen to your own heart as you experience both small and large losses in your own life. You may well be your own best teacher.

MY TRAVEL JOURNAL

1. Who in your life has modeled grief for you? What did you learn? Is there anything you need to unlearn?

2. What other grief experiences have you had besides your current grief? What did you learn from those experiences? What do you hope will be different this time?

SUGGESTED ITINERARY

Take some time to think about what it will be like in Emmaus.

Write down some of the things you hope to experience there.

If there are still obstacles in your way, have a talk with God about them.

Note

1. Myrlene Hamilton, *Turning Points: Moments of Grace, Steps toward Wholeness* (Valley Forge, PA: Judson Press, 1997), 92.

Travel Clothing

As I write these words, I am sitting at my computer wearing comfortable at-home clothes. Stretchy knit pants, T-shirt, and a flannel shirt. *Ed's flannel shirt.* When Ed died, I gave away most of his clothing to other people, those who could make good use of them. But I kept a few items, just to remember him and keep him close. I had done the same thing when my dad died. Right down to the flannel shirt. I was eighteen when my dad died and was bound for college. I didn't have a lot of room to carry large mementos with me. But I could pack away a dad-sized flannel shirt and wear it around the dorm. I kept that shirt for many years, wearing it often at home and letting it give me quiet comfort until it was quite literally in shreds. Ed's shirt does the same for me now. Sometimes I don't even think of it as Ed's shirt when I put it on now. But it still warms my heart. It's interesting to me that it wasn't even Ed's favorite shirt. My choosing of that particular shirt was much more about me and my grief than about him and his preferences.

Often one of the most difficult tasks for the survivor is simply this: What do I do with all his stuff? Do I keep it, sell it, give it away? Ed had collected lots of things that were important to him. Some of those things were important to me, too. I kept them (for instance, his many freshwater fly rods). Some were only important to me *with* him (the boat, the saltwater fishing gear). Some were either duplications (his computer) or only of interest to him (his guns, his tools, his clothes). I gave those away or sold them.

What you do with your loved one's possessions (and when) will depend largely on your own situation and needs, but let me suggest what I think are helpful guidelines:

- Keep enough things to both honor your loved one's memory and maintain a sense of closeness. You and your family and friends can have fond thoughts when looking at familiar photos and special items of interest.

- Don't let material things weigh you down. Remember that you are on a journey, and in a sense, you need to "pack lightly." If it's in the way or you don't like it, go ahead and get rid of it. Maybe someone else can make good use of it.

- Don't confuse your loved one with God. Sometimes people create a sort of shrine with pictures and memorabilia. Your loved one deserves to be honored, but only God is to be worshiped.

These guidelines are not only for material things. There are other things that you may have accumulated because of your relationship with your loved one. Ed left me a number of gifts that I will treasure. A love for Labrador retrievers, for instance, and fly fishing. Because of him, I have a better understanding of how people struggle with certain emotional problems, such as anger. I think I have become a better counselor because of his influence. I treasure these gifts.

On the other hand, there are things we did together that I have stopped doing: shopping at the mall, for instance. Ed loved to shop. I loved to shop—*with him*. We often went to the mall for entertainment. But I don't like to shop for myself. Going to the mall intensified my grief. So, I stopped going. I only go now when I absolutely have to.

MY TRAVEL JOURNAL

1. What have you done with your loved one's possessions?

2. What decisions do you still need to make?

SUGGESTED ITINERARY

Perhaps there are some things you have been putting off. Spend a few minutes:

- sorting through boxes
- wading through thank-you notes
- shuffling paperwork

Allow the tears, if they come.

A Road Map for the Journey

When I am driving to a place that I've never been before, I like to check the map before I go. Often I log onto a website that quickly pulls up a map by using the address I supply. There's usually a choice between getting a map or just narrative directions. For me, the map is the best, because it gives me a visual sense of direction while I am driving along. It is extremely helpful in getting me where I want to go, but I have learned to beware. The maps are not always accurate. Sometimes the address is plotted on the wrong side of a major intersection, and I end up going too far or not far enough. Still, the map usually gets me in the general vicinity, and for that I'm grateful. I've learned to use my own good sense along with the map in order to get where I need to go.

A similar thing is true on the road to Emmaus. A number of people have done a good job researching the territory and have drawn up some helpful maps. But beware of following the maps *too closely*. The road to Emmaus is not a straight line, nor is it a simple matter of step one, step two, step three, and you're there. On your journey of grief, there are bound to be some twists and turns, maybe even some detours that the mapmakers did not anticipate. Though there are definitely some common landmarks to be observed, your journey is unique to you. So read the maps, look for landmarks, use your own good sense along the way, and you will get where you need to go. Here are a few maps that may help you.

For most people, the feelings associated with grief do follow a recognizable pattern. It may be helpful to think of this in visual terms. It's like going down the mountain into a deep valley and then climbing back out of the depths into the foothills of the mountain again.

The loss precipitates feelings of sadness, which deepen, and the person gradually "hits bottom" and begins to gradually feel better again. For most people, however, this is not a neat pattern. Some people will stay at the "bottom" longer than others. Many people begin to feel better and then feel worse and go in a sort of uneven zigzag.

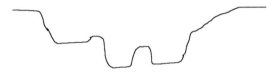

If another loss occurs, the feelings may deepen or repeat. If this happens to you, don't despair! Keep walking the road, and one day soon, you will see that you are climbing out of the valley of the shadow of death. Be aware that you are not returning to the exact same place you left. The journey is forward.

Elisabeth Kübler-Ross, expanding her classic study on death and dying into the realm of grief, has suggested that grieving people move through the same five stages that dying people go through:

Denial

Anger

Bargaining

Depression

Acceptance[1]

Keep in mind that not everyone experiences these stages in the same order. If you are going through them in a different sequence, or if you can't relate to the idea of stages at all, that's okay. Remember that your goal is not to march perfectly to someone else's grief drum (or to march perfectly to your own expectations!). The challenge is to find the transformation and healing that God has for you along the road. That means being responsive to your own experiences, your own feelings, and the wind of God. If the maps help, use them.

Alan Wolfelt, a well-known grief counselor and author, is

adamant that no map for grief exists. He does, however, agree that common themes emerge. He lists six needs of mourning:

1. Accept the reality of the death.
2. Let yourself feel the pain of the loss.
3. Remember the person who died.
4. Develop a new self-identity.
5. Search for meaning.
6. Let others help you—now and always.[2]

Wolfelt makes a distinction between grieving and mourning. Essentially the difference is internal versus external. Grieving is what goes on inside: thoughts, feelings, ideas. Mourning is about what goes on outside, what others may see and experience with you: crying, talking, showing pictures, etc. So the needs for mourning on his list are things that need to be done or accomplished along the way if you are to fully reconcile with your loss. Wolfelt is also emphatic that you don't get *over* a loss; you can, however, become reconciled to it.

Some years ago, I learned yet another way of looking at the process of grief, from a source that I have unfortunately forgotten. It appears to be an adaptation of John Schneider's three phases of discovery. Looking at grief in this way has been incredibly helpful to me, and the nice thing about it is that it's easy to remember. There are three simple stages, or questions:

- What's lost?
- What's left?
- What's next?

The general movement through grief answers these questions in order, but at times you may find yourself all over the map.

During the early phases of the grief process, the most energy is spent on thinking about what has been lost—for example, the person, the relationship, the common activities, the conversations, and the anticipated common future. That's normal, and it's important to give yourself the time to absorb the reality of what's lost and how that has affected your life. Gradually, as you begin to heal, you will move into an emotional space where you look at your life and take stock of what you still have, what is left in life to be valued and appreciated. You will still be sad for what is lost, but you will begin to see your present life in a more positive light. In the "What's next?" phase, you begin to open yourself to new possibilities and a hopeful future.

Though grief itself is not simple, this outline can help you locate yourself on the grief map and perhaps encourage you to continue to move forward. Again, don't despair if you find yourself moving back and forth. That is normal. Sometimes, though, people stay stuck in their grief instead of moving on. They don't make it to the "What's next?" phase. Perhaps it feels too risky to venture out into the future alone. Or maybe you feel that if you allow yourself to move on, it means you no longer care about the person who has died. Or it could be that you have unresolved issues about the relationship that you simply can't let go. All of these are normal feelings and thoughts. You will always have a hole in your life, left by the irreplaceable person who has died, always a certain sadness about the loss. But it's okay to feel better! Embracing the pain of grief honors the person who has died and the relationship you shared. Embracing the future honors life itself.

As I have studied the various grief maps that have been charted and observed my own journey, I have come to describe the journey in terms of three intentional turns that need to be made along the road:

1. Embracing your grief
2. Reorganizing your life
3. Living into God's future

Each one of these turns is an important key to living a whole and purposeful life in the wake of a significant loss. And each one *is* a choice. There are no shortcuts to Emmaus, but if you navigate these turns, I guarantee that you will find your way.

MY TRAVEL JOURNAL

1. Of the various grief maps described, which one is most helpful to you?

2. What are some questions you would like to ask the mapmakers?

SUGGESTED ITINERARY

Using one of the "maps" from pages 38 and 39, create a pictorial description of your journey thus far.

Share the map with someone whom you trust and who will encourage you on your way.

Notes

1. Elisabeth Kübler-Ross and David Kessler, *On Grief and Grieving* (New York: Scribner, 2007), vii, 7–28.

2. Alan Wolfelt, *Understanding Your Grief* (Fort Collins, CO: Companion Press, 2003), 88.

Embracing the Journey

The road to Emmaus is full of feelings, and a primary task for survivors is to work through the feelings associated with grief.

The feeling most generally associated with grief is sadness. But grief is expressed in many other ways as well. Some of those feelings may come as a surprise. The immediate thing that I felt, moments after Ed died, was relief. He went quickly; he didn't have to submit to a hospital bed; he didn't have to have an oxygen tank; he didn't have to be bedridden. He didn't have to suffer. It was over. *Sigh!* I was surprised about that feeling and immediately felt a little guilty. How can I be relieved when my husband has just died? Yet I was.

Guilt is a hard taskmaster at any time, but during times of grief, guilt can feel particularly heavy. Perhaps it's legitimate guilt. If you are in the wrong, it's healthy to take responsibility for your choices and actions (and then accept forgiveness). No one can change the past, and you have limited control over what will happen in the future. God has forgiven you; now it's time to do the hard work of forgiving yourself. You won't be able to move ahead unless you can find a way to resolve this feeling. But what if the guilt is undeserved? You *feel* guilty, but you are *not* guilty. Then you need to face that reality. Let yourself off the guilt hook.

Anger is another tough emotion that often rears its ugly head during grief. You may be angry at the person who died. Maybe he or she was careless, or did not seek medical attention soon enough. Maybe harsh words were said. You may be angry at medical professionals or other family members. You may be angry at God. That's okay. It's all a part of the process. But it may also be a big surprise. Ed's mother died suddenly, just after we had moved to Alaska in 1986. She had a heart attack while sitting in her car in the parking lot of a shopping center. So we made a quick trip back to Tacoma. To everyone's surprise, Dorothy's husband, Fred, was furious. Mostly he was mad at Dorothy, but secondarily he was mad at the rest of the world, especially the family. You see, Dorothy wasn't supposed to die first. She had been taking care of Fred who had been ailing for quite some time, and then she just up and died. It wasn't fair!

Often the anger that comes with grief is transferred or displaced. Instead of being angry directly at the loss itself, you may find yourself getting angry at other things or people. You may even feel angry for no apparent reason. You may find that you express anger that seems out of proportion to the event at hand. If that happens, take a close look at your anger. Ask yourself this: "What is the true source of my anger? What have I lost?"

It can also be helpful to understand that anger is a secondary emotion. Generally, if you feel angry, at the heart you are either afraid, frustrated, or hurt. If you allow yourself to go back to these primary feelings, you may find that you no longer need to be angry, because you can face and resolve the primary feeling.

Anger can also be a signal that something needs to change. I recently read a paraphrase of the familiar Serenity Prayer: *God grant me the serenity to accept the person I cannot change, to change the one I can, and the wisdom to know it's me!* Ask yourself this: "Is there something I need to do differently?"

Another surprise that many experience with their feelings is that they not only grieve for the person who has been lost; they also grieve for what they did not have in the first place. Maybe it was not that great of a marriage. The widowed spouse may grieve the hopes of having a nurturing, loving partner. Maybe your father was distant, so when he dies you think about the things you wish he would have done but didn't. Maybe there was abuse, and you are left with a feeling of unfinished business.

In addition to emotional feelings, many people who are grieving find that physical symptoms emerge, such as headaches, backaches, stomach problems and sleeplessness. Some physical symptoms can be helped by finding a way to openly express your grief in a safe environment. Others can be helped by making a point of choosing a healthy lifestyle: exercise, healthy foods, etc. (these things may have been put on the back burner when you were dealing with your loved one's illness). It's a good idea to see your doctor for a physical checkup if you've recently experienced a great loss. Take care of *you* for a change!

Another thing to note about the physical symptoms is that they can be a signal that you are stuffing your grief instead of processing it. It's well known that many physical ailments have a psychosomatic source. That doesn't mean the illness is not real; it shows that that your body and emotions are connected. If you are not dealing with the emotional journey of grief, your body will react.

It's important to understand that all of the feelings associated with grief are okay. They are real, and they are *your* feelings. Let them be there. The very fact that they are *your* feelings can be very empowering. They can be there without overwhelming you, because they are yours. Still, the burden may feel too heavy. It's okay to ask for help. Talk to a trusted friend, a pastor, a counselor, a grief group, a doctor.

Think of it this way. Feelings (both physical and emotional) are signals that something is going on that needs to be addressed. Don't ignore them. Listen to your feelings, embrace them as your own, and work to understand and resolve them.

If you do ignore them, hear this: they won't just go away. They may go underground and create physical problems. Or they may simply emerge later. I was recently reading an old sermon of Ed's. In it he speaks of his grief over his father's death:

Even today, some twenty-three years later, I remember vividly the day. It was a bright, clear June day. . . . Father's Day seems to stick in my mind. I was in the Cincinnati area on business, staying in the apartment of some friends who were on vacation. The phone rang, and the person on the other end told me that my dad had died suddenly from an aneurysm that had burst in his head. . . . He was fifty-nine years old. I remember the plane trip back to Oregon, the funeral, and the friends and relatives who came to share stories and their grief. I also remember the numbness and disbelief I felt. I didn't even cry. . . . I couldn't seem to feel anything . . . not even as I stood alone by the casket, placed my hand on his, and said good-bye for the last time. A couple of days later I was back in Cincinnati hard at work. Some three years later when I was talking to someone about my dad, what a special guy he had been, how much love he had given to my brother and me and how much I missed him, suddenly I began to weep uncontrollably. Only then did I begin to grieve.

Embracing the journey to Emmaus is mostly about accepting your feelings and making a decision to work through them. You might ask, though, how do I go about doing that? How do I know that I have truly embraced this journey? Like every other journey, it starts with that crucial first step. In this case the first step is a decision to embrace the feelings and to work through them. Then take a look at your own personality and preferences. Would you respond well to a grief group? Then find one. Would you do better speaking to a therapist or a pastor? Take the initiative to set up an appointment. Do you have a circle of friends who understand loss? Create some opportunities to get together and just talk. Do you need time alone? Clear your schedule and give yourself the space (and place!) that will help you to heal.

There are obstacles to walking this road, I don't doubt. The biggest one may be resistance within yourself or among your closest family and friends. People around you are trying to cheer you up; *they* are uncomfortable with the feelings of grief. That is *their* problem, and if that's the case, you may need to cultivate new friendships. That, too, can be an obstacle, especially if you're an introvert. You're afraid to take that first step to call a therapist, walk into a grief group, or introduce yourself to someone. People may think you're weak ("Aren't you feeling better *yet?*"). But do you know what? The opposite is true. Those who embrace their emotions are the strong ones, and those who reach out for help are the ones who will grow. In this, as in everything, God has gone before you and will prepare your way. It's okay to be afraid. Face your fear and keep walking! Time (or lack thereof) may also be an obstacle that keeps you from the road. You have to work; the kids need to be cared for; a multitude of things cry out for your attention. Those are all real concerns. But what about you? Do you want to get better? As an old TV commercial once put it: you're worth it! The same goes for that giant obstacle: money. If you go to a therapist, there will be a cost. Check with your insurance company—maybe it's covered. Check with the counseling center—maybe they have a sliding scale based on income. The key in facing obstacles, whatever they are, is this: don't give up! The road is long and hard, but the transformation that comes along the way is well worth it. Listen to yourself when you are thinking or talking about the obstacles. Are they true obstacles, or are they excuses? Maybe the real obstacle is simply your fear. You are facing the unknown, and that's a scary thing. It's okay to be afraid. Just don't let your fear stop you.

Keep this in mind: everyone experiences loss, but not everyone takes the journey to Emmaus. It's not automatic. Some will make excuses and attempt to keep everything the same. Some will try to "be strong" and try to keep their emotions at bay while engaging in busy work. Others may simply go into denial ("I'm fine!) and stay there. But some will make the courageous choice of walking to Emmaus. How about you? Are you ready to embrace the journey?

Consider this: If you don't go to Emmaus, *where will you go*?

MY TRAVEL JOURNAL

1. What are some of the feelings that you have been experiencing since the loss of your loved one? Have any of those feelings surprised you?

2. What do you need help with?

3. What decisions have you made so far about the journey?

SUGGESTED ITINERARY

Write down all the "feeling" words you can think of (emotions, such as happy or sad).

Try something you've never done before: go bowling, write a poem, eat pistachio ice cream. How do you feel about this new adventure?

The Journey Begins

My cell phone rang just as I was signing the marriage certificate. It was a Saturday afternoon, and I had just finished a backyard wedding at a house a few blocks from home. I was in their kitchen finishing up paperwork. I thought it would be Ed, teasing me about my impeccable sense of timing. Ever since I married Ed's mother and stepfather in 1980, I have had a reputation in the Hamilton family for being late. In Hamiltonese, you are "late" if you arrive just on time. You are supposed to arrive fifteen minutes early. I had asked Dorothy and Fred what time they wanted me to arrive for their marriage ceremony, which was to be at Ed's brother's home. They said "one o'clock." So I arrived at one o'clock, only to discover that they were stewing about me being late.

On this particular Saturday, it was déjà vu all over again. I had told the couple that I lived in the neighborhood and that I would be there at about a quarter to one for the wedding at 1:00. At about 12:30, the bride's sister-in-law panicked and called my office. She called the emergency number listed on our answering machine, which was Ed's pager. When I arrived at the house for the wedding, she mentioned that she had spoken to Ed. So when my cell phone rang after the wedding, I was ready for him to razz me. But it wasn't Ed. It was my secretary with a very terse message. Ed had collapsed during the class he was teaching and had been taken to a nearby hospital. End of message.

Ed and I had both known that something was coming. He hadn't been right for a couple of weeks. He had some motor difficulties when he was typing and some cognitive dysfunction. This was Saturday, and he had just been to his doctor on Friday to talk about his strange symptoms. The doctor had recommended a brain MRI, which was scheduled for Monday.

When I got the phone call, I called my friend Michelle to come and watch our dogs, one of whom was the eight-week-old chocolate Lab whom we had named Amazing Grace and I raced to the hospital. Both of Ed's parents had died suddenly, his father of a brain aneurysm and his mother of a heart attack. I knew I needed to be ready for anything. As I headed up the Garden State Parkway, I turned on my tape player. The first song to play was "It Is Well with My Soul." Even with that encouragement, it was the longest drive I have ever taken.

When I got to the emergency room, Ed was awake and alert. He described what had happened to him, saying that he had lost mobility on one side, and was regaining his ability to use his arm and leg. The first tentative diagnosis was stroke. But subsequent tests showed a mass in his brain. Additional scans later showed a mass in his lung as well. Lung cancer had metastasized to his brain. The brain tumor had caused a seizure, hence the collapse. And it was the brain tumor that had given him the strange symptoms of the previous couple of weeks. It was a lot to absorb, and we had to absorb it fast because we had significant decisions to make.

Within two weeks, he had brain surgery to remove the tumor. Miraculously, that tumor was completely removed, and he had no lingering symptoms. Chemotherapy for the lung tumor began immediately and continued for the next year and a half. For the first nine months he was banned from driving because of the seizure. He had numerous MRIs, CT scans, and PET scans. He had radiation and radiosurgery and two lengthy hospital stays because of infection. Finally, the doctor said, "Enough." Then Ed went under hospice care, and within a week he died.

Then *my* journey began.

MY TRAVEL JOURNAL

1. What were some of the events surrounding your loved one's death?
2. What are some of your still-unresolved feelings?

SUGGESTED ITINERARY

Get out an old photo album and page through it.
Give yourself a hug. And another.

Holy Darkness

It's often true that a poem or a song or a picture communicates truth and emotion far better and quicker than many words in a narrative. The following song by Dan Schutte is one that communicates great meaning to me, and I hope it will to you as well. Think of it as God speaking to you into the dark night of your soul. Don't just read it; drink it in, and let it seep into your heart as you read it and ponder its meaning for you.

Refrain
Holy darkness, blessed night,
heaven's answer hidden from our sight.
As we await you, O God of silence,
we embrace your holy night.

1. I have tried you in fires of affliction;
I have taught your soul to grieve.
In the barren soil of your loneliness,
there I will plant my seed.

2. I have taught you the price of compassion;
you have stood before the grave.
Though my love can seem
like a raging storm,
this is the love that saves.

3. Were you there
when I raised up the mountains?
Can you guide the morning star?
Does the hawk take flight
when you give command?
Why do you doubt my pow'r?

4. In your deepest hour of darkness
I will give you wealth untold.
When the silence stills your spirit,
will my riches fill your soul.

5. As the watchman waits for morning,
and the bride awaits her groom,
so we wait to hear your footsteps
as we rest beneath your moon.[1]

MY TRAVEL JOURNAL

1. Did the song touch your heart? Describe your feelings
and thoughts.

2. What other music or art form helps you in your grief?

SUGGESTED ITINERARY

Practice a silent prayer: Sit in a comfortable chair with your
hands in your lap. Turn your palms down to symbolize
sending away the negative energy you feel. Turn palms up
to indicate your surrender to God and your readiness to
receive all God has to give you. Repeat this several times.

Read Psalm 23.

Note

1. Daniel L. Schutte, *Holy Darkness* (Portland, OR: Oregon Catholic Press,
1988, 1989). Reprinted with permission of the publisher.

Eric's Story

A day before Adrianne died, she called her husband over to her for a conversation. "I want to talk to you about your new wife," she said.

"I don't need a new wife," Eric countered. "I need to take care of the wife I have."

"But soon you'll be needing a new wife," she insisted. "But," she cautioned, "stay away from the man-traps!"

Adrianne was famous for her humor, so Eric thought she was joking. But this time she was dead serious. She knew she was dying, and soon. And she wanted to give him one last gift before she left him: Permission to move on without guilt. After Adrianne's death, Eric learned that she had also communicated this sentiment to one of their daughters and to a friend at church.

This conversation was symbolic of Eric and Adrianne's relationship. Intimate, supportive, straightforward, laced with humor. "She was my first real girlfriend, from when she picked me out when she was twelve," Eric says. "We grew together for a large portion of our lives." She was soft and accommodating yet also a very self-determined person. But after she was diagnosed with Hodgkin's lymphoma at the age of thirty-three, she became "like stainless steel—extremely strong." It was early 1973, a time of new discoveries for treating Hodgkin's. The new treatment was radiation. The good news was the Hodgkin's was cured. She was able to continue teaching kindergarten, to see her three children grow up, and to see all but one of seven grandchildren grow and develop. The bad news was that the radiation left a mark that later showed up in severe nerve damage, lung damage, and sarcoma. For many years, she suffered increasing loss of motor control, particularly in her left arm. At one point she was (inaccurately) diagnosed with congestive heart failure. In fact, she had pulmonary edema resulting from her radiation-scarred lungs' inability to remove fluid, a condition that recurred and got more severe until her death. She was in and out of the hospital repeated times, with attempts to accurately diagnose and treat her symptoms. Finally, thirty-two years after her initial diagnosis of Hodgkin's, she had had enough. She would have no more diagnosis and no more treatments. She was scheduled to enter a hospice program the day she died.

On the day before she died, Adrianne was playing a game of Scrabble with their daughter Laurie. After lunch, she collapsed. Eric gave her some oxygen and called the first-aid squad, who took her to the local hospital. She revived sufficiently to reassure everyone that it would be okay; she would be back home tomorrow. After spending time with various members of the family, she sent everyone home except her sister Carol, who stayed with her through the night. During the night, she went into cardiac arrest and was resuscitated and put on a ventilator. Eric was initially shocked at this because the hospital had on file both a living will and a *do not resuscitate* order. Reflecting upon this later, Eric says that it may have been a fortuitous event because most family members were then able to come and say their good-byes. Adrianne could not communicate because of the ventilator and seemed to have little or no motor function. But her heart rate increased whenever a member of the family spoke to her, and that brought them assurance that she heard their expressions of love and their good-byes.

When she died, Eric began "to feel better and way worse at the same time." He immediately felt relieved that she had gone on the journey that they both had known was imminent. At the same time, he felt a great loss and emptiness. They had been happily married for forty-four years. He felt he had done the best he could, but . . . there were lingering doubts and second-guesses that continued to nag at him. *He should have let her go instead of giving her oxygen when she collapsed at home. She would have been happier with that.* Her wish about her death had been to just go to bed at home with him and not wake up—no tubes or wires or ventilators. *He should not have gone home from the hospital— but she was so sure it would be okay!*

When Adrianne died, Eric was in a fog for a time. Two and a half years later, he still describes himself as somewhat confused. She was the organizer, the one to keep track of dates and times and places. Now he has trouble with keeping appointments because she is not there to help him. He sometimes has trouble making decisions, something that was not an issue for him before. And there has been what he calls "a strange split in social contacts." Many of the people who were friends with Eric and Adrianne because of their connection with Adrianne have more or less dropped away, with the notable exception of a few, and his immediate family has gone into a reorganization that has not yet settled out. Adrianne was the center of gravity, the primary initiator of family events, as well as the reconciler of family grievances. Since her death, the family has been in search of a new center of gravity. Some of those tasks have been taken on by their daughter Laurie, but there is still a sense of the family rebuilding itself, trying to understand how to be a family without the glue that held them together. Adrianne was the peacemaker. Without her, he is not sure how to reconcile some of the relationships that seem to have gone adrift.

A major turning point not long after Adrianne died came when Eric began to give credence to her final instructions—that is, to get a new wife. While Adrianne was still with him, he dismissed the idea as being unreasonable and undesirable. He loved *her* and that was that. He had loved her the best he could for forty-four years and would continue to do that whatever the cost. When the reality of her death settled in, he began to think about that conversation in a new way. "I started to think it wasn't such a bad idea," he said. "I wasn't out looking, but it started to seem like a positive thing." He knew he had her blessing to move on. Still, it was a surprise when it happened. In many respects, it was a classic story: two couples had a close relationship and enjoyed each other's company. One spouse in each couple died. The remaining two found love in each other's eyes. A year and a half later, they married. Eric felt complete freedom from the standpoint of his relationship with Adrianne. It was her idea, after all!

Unfortunately, Adrianne's attitude did not prevent some from being dismayed at what appeared to them as a betrayal. It was too soon for them to see Eric in a new relationship. Of course, Adrianne was not there to tell them it was okay, as she had told Eric. They will need to reconcile their own grief in their own time and their own way.

Eric has found comfort and gained spiritual strength as he has observed the faith of those around him. Adrianne's faith was a model for him throughout their marriage. Some months before her death, Adrianne told her doctor (who refused to move her into a hospice program), "I know where I'm going. I just don't know when." That statement was descriptive of her faith. Though she had a brief time of questioning God when she was first diagnosed with Hodgkin's, the rest of her life was spent, as Eric describes it, in a "steely resolve and reliance on God to take her through—and that reliance never left her."

"As time went by," he said, "her faith and her acceptance of the will of God has helped me greatly." And his young grandson, Eric III (E-cubed, Eric calls him) seems to have latched on to a similar faith. He has no doubt where his grandma has gone.

The faith of others has encouraged him, but his own relationship with God has sustained him. On one of many trips to and from New York to Sloan Kettering Hospital, he was driving past Newark Airport when he became overwhelmed by the enormity of their situation. He passed out while he was driving. When he regained consciousness, he was still driving on the turnpike and had a keen sense of *someone* guiding them. "And I was done being overwhelmed. Now, thirty-four years later, I still see the guiding process and am trying to follow the same path that Adrianne followed—that is, God's path."

That path has him very active in his church and in sailing—which for him are very connected. He teaches a sailing class for the church, in which he reminds people that "sailing is dancing with the wind, and God leads." His compassion for other people has emerged as he has taken several people under his wing and given them guidance and support for their personal growth.

Eric has been called Don Quixote by friends and colleagues over the years. He is an intelligent visionary person, an idealist who pursues goals that other people would not bother with. That has led him to a fair amount of frustration in his life. "I still tilt at a lot of windmills," he says. But in light of his experiences with life and death and faith, "Now I have a whole lot better acceptance of the will of God and work harder to *discern* the will of God."

MY TRAVEL JOURNAL

1. What part of Eric's story do you relate to?

2. If you were Eric's friend, what would you do to support him on his journey?

SUGGESTED ITINERARY

Choose an activity that gets you out in nature: sailing, swimming, skiing, biking, running, walking. Feel the wind on your face as God's loving touch.

PART THREE

The Long Road

Strangers on the Road

As the two disciples walk the slow road to Emmaus, recounting their story, trying their best to make sense of their situation, a stranger comes—seemingly out of the blue—to walk with them. The stranger is Jesus, but they do not recognize him, at least not yet. But this stranger has an uncommon ability to understand their situation, to listen carefully to the story, to reflect their concerns, and at times to challenge and even to chide. Their hearts warm to this stranger, even though they do not yet understand the meaning of this encounter.

People today sometimes talk about needing "Jesus with skin on." This comes from the well-known story of a small child who was afraid to go out in the dark to do an errand. His mom encouraged him not to be afraid, because Jesus would be with him. But the boy insisted, "I need someone with skin on!" Because Jesus is not physically present with us but present in the Spirit, people sometimes long for a more tangible expression of God's comfort and love. And God knows that we need this. Along the Emmaus road, watch for strangers who will prove to be Jesus with skin on—for you.

I first encountered the strangers on the road to Emmaus when I was eighteen and my father died. Countless people tried to express their condolences in hundreds of ways. They said how sorry they were and mouthed various spiritual-sounding platitudes. Their hearts were in the right place, I suppose, and I have a hunch that they also felt a lot of awkwardness in trying to communicate their concern. Maybe they were so uncomfortable with the pain of the situation that they tried to cover it with noise. But there were a few who did not do that. One notable example was Auntie Dori, my father's unmarried sister, who lives in Minneapolis. Usually when she came to South Dakota, she stayed with her sister, my Auntie Marlys, but this time she stayed with us. And she didn't say all those flowery things that other people were saying. She was just there, with us, for us. And that did more for me than all the rest combined. One thing that she did say echoes to this day: "You were his favorite, weren't you?" Well, I had never thought about that. But he was *my* favorite Daddy. I tagged along with him while he was doing his chores, begged him to go fishing, and in other ways made a pest of myself. Maybe he liked it. One thing for sure, he never complained about it.

Some months before Ed's death, a friend from a former parish, Marilyn, started to wonder where I was and what I was doing. So, she "Googled" my name on the Internet. It was fun to hear from her after so many years, and it proved to be a godsend. I told her about Ed's diagnosis and treatment. When I had last talked to Marilyn, she and her first husband were divorcing. She e-mailed me a thumbnail sketch of her life since then. She was now married to her third husband, John. Her second husband had died of lung cancer. Go figure. She was able to share with me, as few others could, what it was like for her and for her husband, both during his treatment and after his death. She also told me stories, many of them humorous, like this one: After her husband was cremated, she placed some of his ashes in a little vial and wore it as a necklace. One day a woman asked her what that was. Marilyn said, "It's my husband's ashes." The woman's eyes widened as she asked, "Was he a very *small* man?" Marilyn was also uniquely able to challenge my thinking after Ed died: Have you done anything yet that Ed wouldn't approve of? (Yes.) What are you getting Ed for Christmas? (Hadn't really thought about it.)

My relationship with Brenda began just a week before Ed died. I had met her on a few other occasions, but neither of us had really "clicked" with each other. Brenda was the wife of a denominational executive and friend, Bill Jordan. On the Friday evening, a week before Ed died, we were at a mutual colleague's home for dinner. During the dinner, I was quite worried about how Ed was doing, as it was obvious his health was failing. But what I also noticed was that Brenda didn't miss a thing. I got the distinct impression that she was seeing more than I could see. Indeed she was, and it was, because her first husband had died from lung cancer. She recognized what Ed was experiencing, and she empathized with my situation completely. Brenda came alongside me on my Emmaus road, told me her story as she listened to mine, and provided a shoulder that was far stronger than her slight frame would suggest. Both she and her husband, Bill, started attending my church, making it clear that my "Jesus with skin on" was present.

I had known Michelle for several years. Both Ed and I had warmed to her instantly when she started attending our church, and our friendship grew as her participation in the church increased. During Ed's illness, she stayed close, available to dog sit, often at a moment's notice, or just to sit and talk. Though she and I had never talked about it, she instinctively knew that she was the one person whom I would allow to come and sit with me in my deepest grief. When Ed died, she came every day for at least a week and stayed throughout the evening. Little was said. It was simply her presence that I needed.

There were myriad others who stepped alongside for a moment or longer, to lend support or to do menial tasks. Candy and Bill stepped in to preach and lead worship; Anne helped sort through clothes and files; Priscilla and others brought food; and the list goes on. What I hope I am communicating by profiling these people is that God knew what I needed before I did, and God knows your need as well. Look and listen for the strangers who come alongside to walk with you on the road. Let them do their work of love in your life, and marvel at the grace of God.

That doesn't mean that you have to accept everything that everyone wants to do. Not at all. In fact, I encourage you to maintain your boundaries. If you don't need what someone has to offer, say so—as kindly as you can. If there's something else you need done that you think that person could do, say so. Grief is one of those times when it's possible to feel as if people are invading your space, and you may not feel as if you have the strength to be assertive. But try. Reclaim your boundaries, and take the time you need to be alone. Get the rest you need, and spend those quiet moments with your feelings. But don't turn into a recluse, either, or you may miss out on the very help you need. Stay in touch with the people who care about you and whom you trust. Be open to new relationships that may become a source of strength and growth. You may find that you begin to notice people whom you had not really noticed before. The person you have just lost, especially if that person was your spouse or a very close family member, greatly influenced how you spent your time, perhaps even how you perceived yourself. That is different now, and while there is great pain in that loss, there is also marvelous potential to discover new gifts, try new adventures, and perhaps even perceive a new you.

A wonderful story came out of the tragic tsunami of December 2004. A year-old hippopotamus was washed down the Sadaki River into the ocean; it then washed up on shore. He was rescued by some park rangers and taken to an animal park. There he became almost instantly bonded with a 120-year-old tortoise named Mzee (in Swahili, this means "old man"). The old man tortoise and Owen, the young hippo, quickly became family. An unlikely pair, you say? Indeed. But the aged tortoise was just the medicine that young Owen needed!

My advice for those who are trying to be Jesus with skin on for their grieving friends and family is this: speak little; listen much; be present. Cultivate a tolerance for silence. Let the grieving person tell you what he or she needs.

MY TRAVEL JOURNAL

1. Who are some of the strangers on the road with you?

2. Have some people made thoughtless or hurtful comments? Take your feelings to God.

SUGGESTED ITINERARY

Write a thank-you note to one or more of the people who have been Jesus with skin on for you.

Take a nap.

A Spiritual Journey

It has been said that people die the way they live. That was certainly true for Ed. Ed lived hard and fast. He didn't like to dilly-dally around. Yes, you could say he was impatient! He continued to work in the midst of his cancer treatment, barely pausing to recover from his brain surgery. He did have to reduce his workload to part-time, but he continued to preach and continued with what had become his first love in ministry, counseling people involved in domestic violence. He refused to stop. In fact, he had appointments in his book for the day he died. On the day the doctor said he needed hospice care, his first question was, "Can I drive?" To his dismay, the answer was, "No." But he could still interact with people, and interact he did, until the last couple of days when he began to retreat into himself and talk less and less.

As his traveling companion, I was left somewhat breathless by his rapid decline and death. But the journey was also very intimate and spiritual in nature. Being with him in his death has changed me and changed my perceptions about death, and life too. I've been a Christian since I was a small child, and as such I have claimed a belief in resurrection life. But eternity seemed very far away, and death seemed alien from human life. Not anymore. A small window opened up during the days surrounding his death that made me glimpse eternity in a way that was profound and that transformed my emotional response to death. The only way I can explain is to tell the story.

It was January 2004, a year and a half since Ed's diagnosis. He had been through countless doctors' visits, four extended hospital stays, brain surgery, too many chemo treatments to count, along with radiation and radiosurgery. In spite of all that, the cancer persisted. For a time, the tumor in his lung stayed constant, but the cancer never did go into remission. Now, at the beginning of '04, it was clear that the cancer was spreading widely.

On January 4, a Sunday, a woman in the congregation told me about a recurrent dream that she had been having. It was so persistent that she was even seeing this dream (I would tend to call it a vision) while awake. She saw what she described as a tree, with a variety of church people gathered around Ed and "your black dog." The woman knew that we had Labradors but did not know their names. Spike, nearly fourteen, was the black dog. She asked me what it might mean. I didn't say what instantly came to mind, which was that both Ed and Spike were dying. Instead, I said that maybe God was telling us to have a special prayer time for Ed at church. Well, maybe God *was* saying that! She agreed that was a good idea, and I set the date for this special time for two weeks hence, to accommodate the schedules of some of the people in the dream.

Ed started telling me that he felt "as weak as a kitten." That became obvious as he began to weaken and fall for no apparent reason. On January 5 he had an appointment in New York City for an MRI. Ed fell while trying to rush across the street from the ferry to catch a cab. In the ensuing two weeks, he had a CT and PET scan locally and another trip to New York (without incident). On Friday, January 16, we had dinner at the home of a colleague about a half hour away. I was reluctant to go because of his weakness, but he was adamant that we needed to be there, so we went, despite the fact that he fell at home while getting ready to go. Those present at the dinner could see that he was failing, though he attempted to keep up a good front. But I think Ed was right—we needed to be there, not so much for him as for me as it turned out. That was the evening that I connected with Brenda who became one of my true anchors in the grief process.

The next Sunday, January 18, we had the special prayers in church for Ed. His appointment with his local oncologist was that following Tuesday. We had brought the films from the recent CT and PET scans with us. We had seen enough of these reports to see that the prognosis was not good. The doctor didn't even look at the films. He had gotten a report from the radiologist, and that was all he needed. He abruptly said it was time for Ed to go into hospice. Now, we had known that this time would come. But since the doctor had not even mentioned hospice in previous visits, we were shocked. But the doctor recognized that I needed more help at home, and he saw the truth of what was going on with Ed. "You are slowly dying," he said. Ed, who had approached the previous year and a half as a battle to be fought, said, "But how can I fight now?" The doctor said bluntly, "The fight is over. Rest." Ed asked him how much time he had left. The doctor suggested that we think in terms of weeks, not months. Intake for hospice was set for Thursday at our home.

On the way home, Ed called our friend Bill. His opening words were, "I'm not going to make it." He called his brother in Tacoma, and later that day, his two daughters. I called my family as well. On the following evening, Wednesday, he began a physical nose-dive, suddenly unable to get around the house well by himself. I was afraid I could not handle him physically, so I called the hospice service. They could not come out because we were not yet signed up with them, but the nurse gave me some tips that got me through the night with him. On Thursday, he was feeling a little better and kept a lunch date with his friend Dave, who was the one person I trusted at that point to be able to support him if he started to fall. The hospice people were there when he got home, along with another friend, Anne, who had been a strong supporter and frequent chauffeur. When the nurse asked him what he needed, he said "just get rid of the death rattle." He had been with enough dying people to recognize the significance in the changes in his breathing. When the nurse reviewed his medications, she quickly tossed out the ones that "we don't need anymore," like cholesterol medication, which became a huge reality check for me. Dying people don't need to worry about their cholesterol.

That evening, Dave came back to sit with Ed while I was leading a Bible study. Because of his labored breathing, he slept in his chair all night. The next day, he was communicative but seemed to be losing the energy needed for conversation. Our hospice chaplain friend, Mary, came for a visit, as did Bill. Ed began to use a "thumbs-up" expression and a smile at times when he did not have the energy to expend on words. At some point during the day, I felt like I had to talk to him about his departure, which was the way I was beginning to feel about his death. He was leaving me. We had been companions for twenty-two years, had shared everything, and now he was going to a place I could not go. And the one who had always told me everything about everything now could not describe what was happening to him, except in brief phrases or a look. Or a thumbs-up. I told him that I was proud of him for what he had done with his life, and that I loved him. I didn't want him to go, but I knew that he had to, and that I would be okay. It was okay. Of course, I didn't *feel* okay, but that's a story for another page of this book.

I've since read that many people stop eating and drinking in the days before their death. Not Ed! He loved food. I served him tuna noodle casserole with apple pie for dessert, and he ate it all with enthusiasm, though he needed a little help from me. That night, he tried to go to sleep in our bed. He had just climbed into bed, and I had turned out the lights, when he got all panicky and said, "The light is too bright." He couldn't breathe well, so he went back out into his chair to sleep. I took a blanket and slept near him, on the couch.

From that point, he never left his chair, except on Saturday morning when he slipped out of the chair onto the floor. I don't know what he was trying to do, because he was unable to say. That was my turning point. I had tried hard up to that point to accommodate his wishes for normalcy, which mainly meant not getting a hospital bed. But I couldn't lift him back onto the chair, and I knew that if he was to be able to stay at home, I needed help. So I did two things. First I called Dave, who came over and lifted Ed back up into his chair. Then I called hospice and asked them to deliver a hospital bed. They promised it for later that day. Ed's words were few that morning. He said, "I feel like such an idiot," when Dave came to help him back into the chair. Earlier, when I came into the room to check on him, he was staring out into space and saying quietly, "home, home." And of course, that was where he was headed.

Late that morning, Anne came to help. I was due to go to a meeting at church, but the events of the morning convinced me I needed to stay. I tried to call both of my stepdaughters, but only reached Tami. When I called Ed's brother Bill, he spoke to Ed, but Ed could not talk back. Bill said he would fly out, but I told him I didn't think he could make it in time, and I was right. It was just about noon when Ed rather quietly moved from this life into the next. It wasn't anything like I thought it would be. It was not alien or strange or repulsive. Just a profound movement in time and eternity. He gasped as if he were going to vomit, and Anne called for me. I came with a towel and sat with him as he took a few more gasps and then stopped breathing. I kissed him and said, "I'll see you in the morning." That was our usual "good-night" message to each other.

Keeping vigil all morning were our three Labradors: Spike, almost fourteen (black); Misty, five (yellow); and Grace, almost two (chocolate). Misty was across the room from Ed, by the sliding glass door, with Spike sprawled in the doorway into the kitchen. Grace was planted right by Ed's feet. All were alert, watching, until after he died. Then, they just flattened out and went to sleep, obviously well aware of what had just transpired. When I finally fell into bed that night, after myriad conversations and a visit to the funeral home, Spike climbed awkwardly onto the bed with me. He hadn't done that for months, because of arthritic joints. But he was going to take care of Mom! Sometime in the middle of that first night alone, I dreamed that I was in a strange place, a rooming house of sorts with bunk beds all around. I was on a lower bunk, and strongly felt God's presence and Ed's. A warm, yellow glow enveloped me. I felt completely wrapped in love, and sensed that my relationship with Ed was somehow sealed inside me at that moment.

Some days later I got a call from Mike, a colleague of Ed's in domestic violence counseling. Mike shared a dream that he had the night after the viewing. Ed had come to him in the middle of a car racing event. He said nothing but just walked toward Mike with a big smile and "thumbs-up." Mike commented that Ed was wearing a tan jacket. When Mike told me about the dream, I told him about Ed's "thumbs-up" greetings during the last couple of days of his life. Both Mike and I knew that this was not a typical expression for Ed to use, and that made it all the more striking, and gave us both goose bumps.

It was on Sunday, February 8, two weeks after Ed died, that I took all three dogs for a walk in the woods. A little later in the day, Spike had what appeared to be a seizure, and with the help of my friend Michelle, I loaded him up and took him to emergency. Two days later he died.

A few days later, I was telling our session (church board) about some of the dreams that people had experienced. One of the session members asked what color coat Ed was wearing in Mike's dream. I told him. He said, "I had one, too," and he proceeded to describe a dream in which Ed encouraged him about his work with the church building project.

In Celtic spirituality, there is talk about "thin places." Thin places are places/times where the boundary between this world and eternity seems to melt away. I now know what they mean, though I can't begin to explain it. I do know that it's not something you can conjure up. It's something that just happens in a particular place and time through the grace of God. Many people describe unusual occurrences at the time of a loved one's death. A pet cries or howls. There is a breeze, apparently from nowhere. I have heard stories that nurses describe, seeing a group of people in a patient's room late at night well after visitor's hours, then upon a second look, the people are gone. And the patient has died!

My friend Elaine, whose story is told later in this book, says that when her husband Dan died, her son Chris observed the spinning rush of a wind. Her daughter Lisa commented that near the date of her father's death, she saw her first shooting star. The day after Dan's funeral, after everyone had gone home, Elaine was working on some bills in the kitchen. Suddenly a gust of wind came through the yard, picking up the barbecue grill that was in a protected corner of the deck. The grill flew off the deck onto the ground. Nothing else in her yard, or the entire neighborhood, had been blown about. Elaine jokes that Dan came and tossed it aside because Elaine would never use it!

I am convinced that if we are going to come to grips with both grief and recovery, then we are going to have to first come to grips with our experience of death itself. In this world in which we live, death is so often a clinical thing—something that happens in the sterile environment of a hospital or nursing home. Family members may or may not be present when the person dies, and even when present they may not feel intimately connected to the event due to all the medical procedures and personnel. I didn't think that I could handle having Ed die at home. I was wrong. He died at home simply because that was where he wanted to be. For me, it was a profound step into an understanding of life and death that I could not have had otherwise. I am grateful for the experience.

MY TRAVEL JOURNAL

1. Did anything unusual occur around your loved one's death?

2. What is your attitude toward the process of dying?

3. What are some of your questions about the spiritual nature of death? Where will you go to answer them?

SUGGESTED ITINERARY

Make a pilgrimage to the cemetery or to the place where your loved one's ashes are scattered. Say what's on your mind.

A Road with Many Forks

The road to Emmaus is a road with many twists and turns, many forks where decisions must be made and new directions sought. At each fork in the road, there is a good-bye and also a vision of the future. An invitation, if you will. If you accept this two-sided invitation, you will find healing.

The first fork, the first good-bye, is centered about the death itself and the necessary events that surround it. Much of that has to do with relationships. Ed died on a Saturday, and the next day, Sunday, I was of course scheduled to preach. I didn't preach, though my sermon was written. Other people led the service, but I still went because I was not the only one touched by Ed's death; it was an event shared by many people, including the church members. I had the idea that I needed to find a way to symbolically convey that relationship right away. Two of Ed's trademarks were his hats and his ties. He was a natty dresser, and he collected *a lot* of clothes. I scooped up most of his hats and ties and took them with me to church to give out as mementos. Later in the week, I distributed favorite clothing items to his daughters and other items to his brother. People responded to the gifts with the same sense of connection that I felt as I gave them.

A man named Bob, who was making a mid-career change in order to respond to a call to the ministry, was able to wear many of Ed's clothes. As a seminary student, buying new clothes was out of the question, so the suits were highly appreciated. One question I had, however, was, *What am I going to do with his shoes?* One day while Bob was at my house trying on Ed's suits, I asked him what his shoe size was. Size nine, he said. Ed's size. Bob began "walking in Ed's shoes" in more ways than one.

There are other decisions to be made in the early days following the death. Will I have a viewing for my loved one? Will the body be cremated? Both? Will the burial take place immediately, or will I wait for a special time to scatter the ashes? Does anyone else need to be consulted? As in other areas of life, the options have increased in recent years. That can make the time around the death even more stressful because of the confusion created by many choices, and perhaps by the opinions of many people. Talking about these things ahead of time will help you confidently face these decisions. Many people are hesitant to talk to a dying loved one about death, yet such conversations are very freeing. As you make decisions, you will have the peace of knowing that you are doing what your loved one wanted.

I decided a long time ago that I wanted to be cremated and have my ashes scattered on the family farm in South Dakota. I told Ed that. He was far less concerned about what happened to his body after death. He really didn't care. What mattered to him was the spiritual aspect of life beyond death. So, when he died, it was up to me to create a scenario that I would feel good about and that would hopefully be helpful to his extended family as well. Because we had moved many times, we had never adopted a place as permanent home, other than the places where we had grown up. But both of us loved a favorite fishing spot in central Oregon. The Metolius River was a place where Ed had spent much time as a child with his parents and his brother, Bill. It seemed to me that the Metolius was the *place* to go. Cremation was the *way* to go. Because of the nature of the culture here in our community (as well as family coming in from a distance), it also seemed important to have a viewing. So, I did both. First a viewing, then cremation. I waited a year and a half before going to the Metolius with Ed's extended family to scatter his ashes. Summer was the best time to make that pilgrimage, and I simply wasn't ready to do it the first summer after his death. So I waited.

In one sense, these are all very practical matters, but they are all part of the grief process as well. Each decision is a part of saying good-bye; each event contributes to the eventual resolution of the feelings that come with the good-bye. I suggest you be as intentional as possible with each event, moving through the feelings as they come, and moving into the future as each good-bye is said. Involve other family members when it's appropriate. Remember the children and consider their need for closure on their own terms. Kids need to know that they are being listened to, but they may not be ready to talk! Let them be involved to the extent that they *want* to be involved. Make sure that they each have a meaningful memento to carry with them into the future.

The events surrounding the death itself create the biggest fork in the road, the most public good-bye, but there are many others, smaller perhaps, yet all a part of the healing process.

Shortly after Ed died, a friend e-mailed me and asked, "Have you done anything yet that Ed would disapprove of?" I had. I hadn't thought of that as any kind of universal experience. I just became quickly aware that whatever decisions were going to be made would have to be made by me. I jokingly replied that I had said to Ed in my mind, "You no longer have a vote in this." I wasn't being mean, just practical. I needed to make decisions that I could live with, whether or not he would approve.

In other areas, though, I continued to live as if he were still with me. I was, in a sense, going on autopilot. This was particularly true in relationships. One particular relationship had become very important to him, in a father-daughter sort of way, that resulted in her being very involved in his medical appointments and in meeting a great deal of his transportation needs. After Ed died, she and I (and her family) continued to relate closely, until I finally realized—in a way that was quite painful for both of us—that maintaining the relationship at that level was not appropriate for me. The father-daughter relationship was between the two of them. She and I did not share the same kind of relationship. And Ed was gone. Painfully, we both moved on.

Then there was the day I stopped wearing earplugs to bed. Ed had been a snorer, and the earplugs helped me get a good night's sleep. The snorer was gone, and I didn't need them anymore. And then there was the day that I got out the hose and added water to the water bed. The required water level for two people in a water bed is lower than for one. Ed was gone, so I filled it up.

I found that I needed to do some very physical things to work out my grief at certain points. I looked around the house and saw many things that needed to be changed. The garage needed to be cleaned. Well, it had needed to be cleaned for a very long time, but going and mucking about in the garage helped me to work out externally some of the housecleaning that was going on inside of me. I wanted to make some minor changes/improvements to the kitchen and entry, so I hired someone to do that. The biggest thing, though, was Ed's study. I had given away his computer and most of the furniture. So the room was sitting mostly empty, but cluttered, with the door closed. It bugged me to no end. *I've got to do something*, I said to myself. So I made it into a spare bedroom. I left the fly-fishing wallpaper intact and used the existing bookcases, but I bought a queen-sized bed and new, colorful bedding. The transformation of the room was energizing. I liked just walking into the room and feeling the energy that seemed to exude from it. It was not empty anymore. Nor was it devoid of Ed. But it had a purpose that made sense in both the present and future use.

As Ed's birthday approached, people asked me if I was going to do anything to mark the day. Frankly, I had not planned to do anything. But when the day came, it seemed appropriate to do something. So I cleaned off his workbench in the garage. Well, *he* wasn't going to do it! And it was time I learned what was on it.

During the first few months after Ed's death, I was meeting regularly with Mary, my hospice chaplain friend. Those conversations were incredibly helpful, but then Mary told me she was moving away to a new call. Once again I thought, *I've got to do something*. I didn't feel as though I was a good candidate for a grief group at the time, but I felt as if I could use some help working through my feelings. So I sought and found a therapist who turned out to be just the right person for me. I told her that I wanted to deal with my feelings so that I could be whole and healthy and move on with the rest of my life. Ruth helped me to do that in some very creative and challenging ways. Being a rather cognitive person, it's easy for me to rationalize feelings instead of dealing with them, but I knew that if I was going to grow into my future whole and healthy, then I needed to embrace the feelings. Little did I know how those feelings would shift and change as the months went on! (More about that later.)

When the time came for the first anniversary of Ed's death, I had wanted to approach that event very privately. I would take the weekend off, I thought, and just stay at home, contemplating and remembering. But certain events in the church and unusual interactions between people indicated that there was some grief work that needed to be done with them as well, so the session (church board) and I agreed that we would arrange for some special events to commemorate that anniversary, to hopefully help people further resolve their own grief. My friend Bill would be preaching, so at least I wouldn't have to preach on that first anniversary weekend. But I would have to be there. As a conclusion to the weekend, I planned a dinner at a local restaurant with the board members and their spouses. Well, sometimes plans go awry. Or you might put this under the column, "God has a sense of humor." On the weekend of that first anniversary, we had one whale of a snowstorm. We almost never cancel our worship services, but we did that Sunday. So, I got my wish after all. I stayed home and quietly contemplated the journey that I was on. But later in the day, the roads were cleared, and we were able to have the dinner as planned. On that weekend I began working on a video that would become the centerpiece of the family event at the Metolius in July.

Each fork in the road, each *I've got to do something*, signaled a deepening of the good-bye and an intensifying of the vision of the future, and at each fork, I made the decision to feel the good-bye and embrace the future.

So often, in the grief experience, people feel helpless, as if grief is simply washing over them in waves and they have no say in the matter. Often the feelings do come in waves, but as in all of life, there are many decisions that we are making in the midst of all that is swirling around us. I want to encourage you to be very aware of this. If you make the basic decision to be intentional about your grief, then you can also face the waves unafraid, knowing that you are headed somewhere (maybe you can learn to surf!). God is involved all along the way, from beginning to end, and God's intent for you is always good. Become a partner with God in your grief. It is an incredible journey. Incredibly painful, yes, but also incredibly healing.

MY TRAVEL JOURNAL

1. When your loved one died, what were some of the first decisions you had to make? How do you feel about those decisions now?

2. What do you need to do right now?

SUGGESTED ITINERARY

Get physical! Clean the garage—dust the furniture—sweep the porch.

Begin to make a plan for the next "anniversary"—whether it's your loved one's birthday or six months after the death or any other important day. Plan how you will mark the day and whom you will invite to be a part of it.

Disarray

My books are in disarray.

I'm the kind of person who organizes according to my own system. (Based on the Myers-Briggs system of understanding personality, I am INTJ—introverted, intuitive, thinking, and judging—which means, among other things, that I am much more comfortable working in a system of my own creation than in someone else's.) Someone else may not be able to find a particular book in my office, but I can. At least I usually can. Normally I have a visual sense of where things are.

One day I was looking for *Pilgrim at Tinker Creek* by Annie Dillard. It's a book that impacted me greatly when I read it, and I wanted to share it with someone. I knew exactly where I had shelved it. Or so I thought. As I scoured the bookshelves at home and at the office, I was dismayed. My books were in disarray. Not only could I *not* find the book I was looking for, but I was no longer sure of my own organization either.

My mental picture was gone, or so it seemed. I was determined to find the book, though, so I persisted until I found it. It took days. In the meantime, I scanned my internal being, which was also in disarray. Such is the nature of grief. Everything seems as if it is tossed to the wind, and it's not at all clear how things will settle out.

It's tough for someone like me to embrace such a chaotic state of being. I like things to be decided, done, certain. I am uncomfortable with being on the way to somewhere—I know not where. If I have to go somewhere new, I would rather simply *be* there. But if I want my outcome to be good (and I do), then I need to travel the whole road and not skip over the tough parts.

As I said earlier, those who embrace grief also experience transformation. This means I need to hold tight in the midst of the disarray. Trusting that something good will come of it in the end and not giving up; not giving in to the desire to create order, any order, instead of waiting for God's new design to emerge.

God created a whole world out of chaos. No doubt God can create something good in the midst of my own disarray. If I look at my own history, both recent and long ago, that has been true. In the midst of my faltering grief when my father died, my call to ministry emerged. During my second major bout with grief after Ed died, the transformation was somewhat more earthy, as I gained a new appreciation for my womanhood. Both transformations were at the core of my being, linking me to God.

I commented earlier about the importance of embracing your feelings in the midst of grief, but I want to make one thing very clear. The road of grief is not merely about feeling bad and then feeling better. It's about the very difficult task of reorganization. It's not easy to close off one chapter of your life and begin a new one, but that is the goal. And to get to that goal, you need to be willing to accept—at least for a time—disorganization. If you have entrusted the journey to God, you can also trust this time of disorganization to God as well. God will bring good out of the chaos.

There is a prayer by Pierre Teilhard de Chardin that I often turn to when I am having trouble with living in a time of disarray. I'd like to share it with you. It's called "Patient Trust."

> Above all, trust in the slow work of God.
> We are quite naturally impatient in everything
>   to reach the end without delay.
> We should like to skip the intermediate stages.
> We are impatient of being on the way to something
>   unknown, something new.
> And yet it is the law of all progress
>   that it is made by passing through
>   some stages of instability—
>   and that it may take a very long time.

And so I think it is with you.
    Your ideas mature gradually—let them grow,
    let them shape themselves, without undue haste.
Don't try to force them on,
    as though you could be today what time
    (that is to say, grace and circumstances
    acting on your own good will)
    will make of you tomorrow.

Only God could say what this new spirit
    gradually forming within you will be.
Give Our Lord the benefit of believing
    that his hand is leading you,
and accept the anxiety of feeling yourself
    in suspense and incomplete.[1]

MY TRAVEL JOURNAL

1. Have you experienced periods of chaos during your grief? How do you feel about that? Can you entrust the chaos to God?

2. Look again at the poem. What phrases challenge you or encourage you? Take those thoughts to God.

SUGGESTED ITINERARY

Get out your favorite movie (if you can find it!) and watch it with a friend.

Note

1. Pierre Teilhard de Chardin, "Patient Trust," in *Hearts on Fire: Praying with Jesuits* (St. Louis: The Institute of Jesuit Sources, 1993), 58.

Ambushed

I was headed home on a rainy, late fall afternoon. It was dark and dreary. My left blinker was on as I waited for the oncoming traffic to clear and allow me to make my left turn. Without warning I was jolted by a loud crack as my car lurched forward and my head snapped back onto the headrest. An inattentive driver had rear-ended me. He was sorry, he said, but he just didn't see me. A quick examination of the car and myself showed that all was well, except my emotional state. I knew it wasn't intentional, but I was angry just the same. I could have been hurt. My car could have been crunched.

On the road to Emmaus, you may well experience similar jolts that will make you feel as though you've been ambushed. Things are rolling along, you're feeling better every day, and then wham! You are rear-ended by a memory, a scent, a song, a word. It happened to me one Sunday morning, about five months after Ed had died, just as I was arriving at church. When I pulled into the parking lot, there was Ed's boat—a seventeen-foot Boston Whaler. Now, I knew it would be there, because a friend was starting a summer ministry that would use the boat. The boat and the ministry were being commissioned that day. But when I drove into the parking lot, my heart sank. All the feel-better progress that I had made during the past few months was wiped away in an instant as I sunk in the depths of grief. I didn't want to go to worship. I didn't want to help with the dedication. I just wanted to go home and hide. But of course, I couldn't. I'm the pastor, after all! So I stayed, but I let others take care of the dedication.

A couple of months later, I was startled awake by a phone call at about 12:30 a.m. The voice on the other end of the line was familiar, but I couldn't believe what Margie was saying. "My husband was killed in a motorcycle accident." It was a tragic accident, and Hank's death would affect Margie and her family in dramatic ways. But the jolt that I felt was out of proportion to its relationship to me. In fact, I felt like it was happening *to* me all over again. In a sense it was. I had not felt lonely in the months since Ed's death, but suddenly, sitting up in bed, I started to shake all over. I felt desperately alone. When Ed and I were pastoring together, he had always been the first responder. He thrived on emergencies and loved going to someone's aid no matter what hour of the day or night. I am more the methodical planner type. Emergencies jolt me. And now it was my job to respond.

Several months later, I was jolted again. It was early December, and I was in my car, just driving along, when I started to see other cars with Christmas trees tied to their roofs. I felt a stab of grief. People with husbands and families bring Christmas trees home on the roofs of their cars. But not me. Not this year. The pain lingered as I considered my new widowed state.

These encounters with grief feel like ambushes, but they are no one's fault.

I think it's helpful to understand that grief is not something that one gets "over" like one gets over a cold. It's a road that we travel, and sometimes we pass familiar and painful landmarks. The feelings of grief dissipate, but because the loss is permanent, the grief will always be there in some measure. Familiar sights and sounds can bring back the feelings. But that doesn't mean that you aren't getting better! You are, and the ambush is actually a proof of that. If you hadn't been feeling better, the pain would not have been so obvious. Know that it's normal to experience this kind of grief. Feel the pain, embrace it, and see what it has to tell you. Then let it dissipate as the other feelings have as well, and continue to move forward. You have come a long way!

MY TRAVEL JOURNAL

1. Have you been ambushed by your grief? What happened? How did you respond?

2. How does it feel to hear that grief is not something one "gets over"?

SUGGESTED ITINERARY

Breathe. Breathe out and feel the stress and strain leave your body. Breathe in and consciously welcome in God's love, mercy, peace (and hope!). Repeat.

Tell yourself, "With God's grace, I can do this!"

Blue Christmas

[handwritten margin notes: talk write journal remember Embrace]

Holidays are the toughest. Ask anyone who is on the road to Emmaus. Everyone else is having a "holly jolly Christmas" it seems, and you are down in the dumps. Everybody wants you to have a good time, it seems. *Don't be a downer.* But in the midst of a flurry of upbeat Christmas carols come the strains of a song made famous by Elvis: *"I'll have a blue Christmas without you."* It's about a lost love, but anyone who has experienced a loss of any kind can relate to the mood of that song. Christmas is billed as a time of joy and warm family reunions, but many people have the opposite experience. The season magnifies the tough reality of loss.

The same is true of other holiday or anniversary times, especially during the first year after the loss. You have certain traditions and special thoughts about the holiday. Now everything is different. Everything reminds you of the loss.

There's good news in the midst of this painful season, though. You don't have to follow the Christmas crowd. You can choose a different path. You don't have to be a party animal if you don't feel like it. But you don't have to crawl into a cave until the season is over, either. There are ways to survive and even use the time as a way of healing.

Here are a few practical suggestions for intentionally dealing with Christmas and other holidays:

1. Plan a deliberate way to honor the person who died (displaying photos, sharing memories with friends and family, scrapbooking, sorting through memorabilia).

2. Begin to create new traditions for yourself instead of continuing all the old habits of the season. Are you afraid no one will invite you to dinner? Invite someone to your house instead!

3. Do something that reflects the life passion of the person who died (e.g., make a contribution to their favorite charity).

4. If you don't feel like doing something, don't! Give yourself permission to say no.

MY TRAVEL JOURNAL

1. Have you encountered some holidays on your way to Emmaus? What were your feelings? What did you do?

2. What are some practical ways that you can use the holidays to help you work toward healing?

SUGGESTED ITINERARY

Start your Christmas list. Begin to plan for Christmas, using one of the author's suggestions or an idea of your own.

Dan's Story

"The last five years have been hell," Dan said to me recently. I nodded, because I already knew his story. Five years ago, he lost his thirty-year-old son, Eric, and eight-year-old granddaughter, Lauranna, in a car accident. Five years of grieving have been punctuated by his own brushes with mortality. Just two weeks after their deaths, Dan was diagnosed with prostate cancer, which was successfully treated. A few months ago, he was diagnosed with esophageal cancer, which has been treated with chemotherapy and radiation. "So far so good," he says of the cancer. It has gone into remission, and he's doing well, though he has to live with some lingering effects of the radiation. Of the five-year-old grief, he says, "There's no closin'." Though he has accepted the reality of the loss, he still struggles with the lack of closure. There's so much he doesn't know about the accident, and an insurance lawsuit is still working its way through the legal system. Will the lawsuit give him closure? "It might help a little bit if I can know the facts," he says, "but it won't take away the pain."

Dan describes his son Eric as fun-loving, funny, a comedian, interested in mechanical things, fishing, and people, and sometimes a troublemaker "just like his old man." Theirs was a very close father-son relationship. When Dan and his first wife divorced, three of their five children stayed with Dan, while the other two went with their mother. The youngest of the five, Eric was always close to his dad. That closeness continued into adulthood as Eric forged his own relationships and built his own family. Eight-year-old Lauranna was a smart, loving, affectionate little girl: a "little lady" who liked to wear dressy dresses and special shoes.

The accident happened on June 14, 2002, in the early evening. Eric's wife, Melissa, was driving; Eric was in the passenger seat; and the kids—eight-year-old Lauranna and six-year-old Gregory—were in the backseat of a 1994 Geo Tracker. "A death trap," Dan had called it just weeks before when Eric brought the family to visit Dan and his wife, Nancy. "This car is no good," Dan said. "If you put your family into this car, something bad will happen." He remembers the conversation clearly, and the feeling of dis-ease that went along with it.

It was a misty-foggy evening as the family headed for the graduation of Melissa's younger sister. The car swerved left on a curve, and an oncoming truck hit them on the passenger side. When the paramedics arrived, Eric was revived at least twice and then sent on to a nearby trauma center along with Gregory and Lauranna, while Melissa was taken to a different hospital.

Meanwhile, Dan was at a show with his boss, Jim, in Atlantic City, about an hour from home. While they were there, Jim got a phone call and simply said to Dan, "We have to go home." Dan quizzed him, thinking that Jim had a problem. Finally, Jim broke down and said that Eric had been in an accident, but he didn't know the details. Nancy had called simply to say hurry home. As quickly as they could, they got home, and Dan and Nancy went up to the hospital where Eric and his two children were. It was about 9:30 p.m. when a doctor came and told Dan that Eric had died of multiple internal injuries. "What did you say?" Dan kept saying to the doctor. And then, "I want to see him."

Lauranna was in another part of the hospital, on life support until 4:50 the next morning, when she too was pronounced dead.

"I was shocked, dumbfounded. This can't be happening," Dan said. He couldn't believe it at first. Then, when reality sank in, the hurt came. "It stays with you," he says. "It's still there now, and it's been five years. I don't like it. It hurts."

Sometimes the pain subsides, he says, but then it comes back. Not a day goes by without the memory coming back several times.

In the midst of his grief, though, Dan has found moments of peace. A couple of days after the funeral, Dan was sitting at the table on his back deck, looking at his American flag. In the windless air, the flag hung lifeless on its pole. Then the flag moved, just a little bit, and a moment later there was a "thump!" as if someone had sat down on the other side of the table and slapped a hand on it. Then it happened again. There was a sense of presence that Dan felt was either Eric or Lauranna. Then he felt the physical sensation of being hugged. He told his wife, Nancy, "Eric is here, holding me."

"It felt good," he says now, remembering. For the next half hour Dan spoke to his son, thanking him for the good times they had had together and talking about things he wished he could change. During all this time, Dan noted that the flag was hanging limp in the still air. Suddenly there was a little flutter, as if someone had brushed by. He took that as a sign that the visit was over. "It took a lot of pain out of me to have that little talk," he said. A couple of days later, his stepdaughter Lori and her kids were visiting. Out of the corner of his eye he saw a black and white animal scoot around the shed in the backyard. He warned the family to stay away, in case it was a skunk. Upon closer examination, though, it turned out to be a kitten. His granddaughter Victoria immediately named the kitten Angel. Dan calls it Lala (Eric's pet name for Lauranna), and feels close to Lauranna when the cat snuggles up to him.

The two deaths and two cancer experiences have left their mark on Dan. And it's not all about pain. He often tells me that he now has a mission in life, and he is trying to understand exactly what it is. Though he's not exactly sure about the nature of his mission, he does have some clues. Now, he says, he feels more caring toward people, and more understanding. He has begun to discover and develop spiritual gifts that connect him to people in need—he finds himself praying for people with a new sense of urgency and purpose. As a result of his struggle, he is more in touch with what life is all about. "You can be here today, gone tomorrow. Appreciate what you have. I wake up every morning and say, 'Thank you, God,' for trees, birds, clouds, wind, rain. How precious life is."

One of those precious things is his grandson Gregory, who often says, "Tell me about my father." At age eleven, Gregory is doing well, and he is in many ways the picture of his father, who in turn was the image of Dan. Being with Gregory lets Dan remember the good times with Eric while he builds his relationship with Gregory.

Dan's wife, Nancy, has been at his side through all the events of the past five years, both supporting and encouraging him. Another precious thing is his church. He credits the people in his church for helping him through these five years and helping him to grow closer to Jesus. "I leave it all to Jesus now," he says, "who lifts the pain, at least for a while."

MY TRAVEL JOURNAL

1. What part of Dan's story do you relate to?

2. If you were Dan's friend, what would you do to support him on his journey?

SUGGESTED ITINERARY

Make a list of the people who are precious to you—especially in the wake of your recent loss.

Plan an appreciation event: a movie night, dinner out, a day at the beach. If you're not up to an outing, send a love note or an e-mail just to say, "Thank you for being you."

PART FOUR

The End
of the Road
Is a New
Beginning

The New Beginning

The stranger/Jesus acts as if he intends to go on beyond Emmaus, but Cleopas and the other disciple, true to the hospitable nature of their culture, ask him home for dinner. Just as the meal gets started, their guest picks up a loaf of bread, blesses it, breaks it, and gives it to them. The two disciples are mesmerized by that simple act. There is something familiar about those hands. They watch the hands breaking bread, and memories come flooding back. A few loaves of bread broken for a multitude of people. Gentle, healing hands, touching the sick and making them well. A special meal on Passover night—bread broken by those same hands ("This is my body, broken for you"). Suddenly, in those hands, in that bread, the two disciples recognize Jesus. Just as suddenly, all of the pieces of the puzzle fall together, and the picture is complete. Everything they have learned from Jesus, everything they have seen and experienced, flow into that one moment at the dinner table, and everything that is to come in their future flows from that moment of recognition, of faith.

This is their defining moment, and it transforms them. Jesus is alive!

This story communicates the core truths of Christian faith. The resurrection of Jesus seals his work on the cross and our salvation. In addition, it opens a door for us to experience the resurrection life ourselves. In other words, this story is about conversion. Cleopas and the other disciple become genuine believers in that moment. They understand the nature of Jesus' work, and they understand that they can participate in it.

All of us who read this story can enter into it in the same way, embracing the work of Jesus in our life and experiencing our own conversion.

For those who have experienced a significant loss, the story gains another layer of meaning. In addition to the core truths at the heart of this story that bind us to the Christian faith, there is a sense in which we can experience a transformation every time we walk the Emmaus road. The moment comes when the pieces start to fall together. God's grace and love and power begin somehow to make sense. And the end product is that your eyes are opened and you recognize him. That is, you recognize what God is doing in your life at the present time, and what God is doing has everything to do with life.

Recognition is the key thought here. All along the way, these two disciples were kept from recognizing Jesus. They had to struggle; they had to tell their story; they had to hear Jesus explain the things they needed to know. They had to give up false hopes. They had to grieve. But now it is time to discover that the end of the road is a new beginning. Having struggled to make Jesus into the Messiah that they had wanted him to be, they are now ready to meet Jesus as he really is. They are ready to become the new people God means for them to be. Are you?

Transformation is what the road to Emmaus is all about. It's not just about *feeling better*, though I hope that you feel better already! It's about (1) embracing your grief, (2) reorganizing your life, and (3) living into God's future. For those who walk the Emmaus road, there is a moment of recognition. The stranger on the road has a name, and that name points to the future.

In a previous chapter, I described some of the strangers who came and walked beside me on my Emmaus journey. There is one more. Eric. His story is told on page 52–56. He was no stranger when he stepped beside me on the road, but the meeting was a revelation just the same. Ed and I had met Eric and his wife, Adrianne, when we first moved to Bayville, and they were among the first to join our fledgling congregation. We became friends and enjoyed spending time together. Eric is a lifelong sailor, and one of his goals was to teach us both how to sail. Ed picked it up intuitively. I was more deliberate in my attempt. I struggled and pretty much gave it up, while Ed took every opportunity to go out on Eric's boat. After Ed died, I still spent time with Eric and Adrianne. Then, a little more than a year after Ed died, Adrianne also died.

With both Ed and Adrianne gone, I started to have strange feelings about being around Eric. I remember thinking, "Now I'm not going to get to spend time with him anymore, because it would be too awkward." The funny feelings intensified and proved to be mutual. Sparks flew. We both sensed an attraction that had never been there before.

The problem was that I was Eric's pastor, and there were rules against a pastor dating a member of the congregation—or so I thought. So, I surreptitiously researched the presbytery rule book and found out that I was wrong. It wasn't against the rules, just a bit complicated. Certain notifications had to be made, certain *i*'s dotted and *t*'s crossed. But it wasn't out of the picture as I had thought. When I made that discovery, and Eric and I confided in each other that the magnetism was shared, I felt a surge of feeling for him that was incredibly strong. I recognized that God was doing something new in my life, something both unexpected and marvelous. Something that transformed me.

I need to tell you that I was not out looking for a man. I had come to a point of acceptance of my solitary state, and I felt as if I was doing okay in it. I was still dealing with grief issues, but I was liking my life, enjoying my friends, my home, my dogs.

Running parallel with my new relationship was a strange new feeling about my role as a pastor. I had been in this congregation, first with Ed, and now solo, for close to twelve years. That is a rather long-term pastorate in today's world. I had assumed that I would be leaving for a new call before too long. I didn't want to leave the congregation in the lurch (we were planning to build), but I didn't want to stay too long, either. Besides, pastors move! That's the nature of the ministry, and in my case, I had moved rather frequently. Until now. I had begun to sense that I wasn't going anywhere, and that was an odd feeling. A new picture of myself was emerging, one that dovetailed with my relationship (fast-moving toward marriage) with a man who is very settled in this community. My struggle to accept this may sound strange, since I had already lived here for twelve years, but for twelve years, I had lived with my bags packed, so to speak. *Another move will come,* I thought. *If not now, maybe next year, or the next.* And now, I'm staying. The internal change that this has created is dizzying. And a little scary. Funny, that's how I used to feel about moving—a little nervous and scared. Now I feel that same agitation about staying. But it's God's movement in my life, so I know it will come out right in the end.

So does that mean my grief is over now that I have a new love in my life? Hardly. As Eric said to me early on in our relationship, his grief over Adrianne's death and his love for me "are two different things entirely." My friend Brenda, who lost her first husband to lung cancer and later married Bill, said the same thing. I asked her whether the fact of being happily married takes away the original grief. She said no, they are two separate realities. As my marriage to Eric approached, I found myself in a kind of a grief warp. Making a new commitment to a new person intensified the good-bye that I had been saying to Ed for more than two years. A new relationship does not (should not) replace the old. It is something new. The road of grief still needs to be walked, and the good news for us is that Eric and I have been able to walk with each other through some of the painful events.

So, the end of the Emmaus road is not an end, but a new beginning. What will it be for you? A new relationship? Perhaps, but don't count on that. Maybe God has something else in mind. A new calling, a new adventure, a new way to offer your gifts to the world. A new way to engage with all the wonder in God's creation. Most certainly a new way of experiencing yourself and those around you, if you open yourself to it.

Openness is the key, I believe. A kind of hospitality toward newness. Encourage the stranger to linger a while as Cleopas and his companion did. Open your mind and heart to a new way of perceiving your life. Let God break the bread of life at your supper table and reveal himself to you.

MY TRAVEL JOURNAL

1. Have you experienced a new beginning on the road to Emmaus?

2. How do you feel about it?

SUGGESTED ITINERARY

Look out your window and notice the season. Step outside and recognize the signs of life that are there.

Come back inside and do a heart-check. Write down the signs of life that you observe in *you*. If you need help, ask a good friend to point out some hopeful changes in you.

Enjoy the Scenery

I'll never forget Mildred. Though I had watched numerous people experience grief, I had never stopped to analyze what I was seeing—until Mildred. That's because Mildred broke the mold. I had seen sadness and gradual recovery as people returned to their lives more or less healed from the wounds of grief. I had seen some people get stuck in their grief and stay locked into the past. I had seen others try to ignore their grief and just get on with life. But Mildred was different. For her, grief was a series of surprising discoveries. About herself.

I met Mildred just a couple of years after I entered the ministry. Her husband had died suddenly from a massive heart attack. They were both in their sixties. Edgar was a Presbyterian minister who had just decided to go into semi-retirement while serving as a stated supply pastor for a small congregation. I got to know Mildred because I was the pastor to fill his position after he died. Mildred felt all the sadness, the shock, the dismay, the disbelief that other people feel when they lose their spouses. But something else rather quickly took over. She was on a new road, and she liked it. It was a new adventure. It surprised her greatly.

I remember her talking to me about her financial concerns. After Edgar died, Mildred worried that she would be in financial ruin. She had essentially given herself to his ministry in the "whither thou goest" mode of marriage. She had been happy with that, but it made her feel uneasy when he died. What would she do to survive? But when she got his death benefits, she was pleasantly surprised. She received a lump sum payment, along with monthly survivor payments. More than she expected. She would never be rich, but she could live on that!

Then she made another interesting discovery. Her husband had been a pipe smoker, and tended to leave a trail of tobacco here and there. She was glad not to have to clean up after him anymore! She could have a clean, smokefree environment, and she could do it without feeling guilty.

She continued to make more discoveries about herself. She was a gifted woman, something that I think she had not entirely paid attention to in her marriage. And she liked to travel. Mildred was elected an elder in our congregation, and she served well. She also saved up some money and went to visit her missionary children in Nepal.

Mildred's daughter Marcia says this: "After my mother went to Nepal, she went through tremendous struggle as she grieved for my father and the loss of her meaning as she experienced it up to then. This resulted in tremendous growth spiritually and vocationally, even while she continued to grieve for my father. She both became more of a person in her own right and missed the love of her life."

The obvious lesson that I learned from Mildred is that it's okay to enjoy life after you have lost a loved one. At first it may not seem possible. It may even seem disrespectful, but it's not.

What often happens in close relationships, especially marriage, is that the partners give up certain parts of themselves *because of* or *for* the other person. That sort of compromise may have helped them sustain intimacy and cope with their differences. But when the other person is gone, then what? Are there interests that you've set aside or skills that you have not yet discovered? Maybe even a calling from God that awaits you in Emmaus? It's okay to make these discoveries. There's a whole world out there. Go see.

MY TRAVEL JOURNAL

1. What new discoveries are you making in the aftermath of your loved one's death?

2. When was the last time you laughed—really hard?

SUGGESTED ITINERARY

Make a list of things you enjoy doing—or think you would enjoy.

Make a plan to go and do at least one thing on the list.

Survivors

"Well, we cheated death again." Ed often made that comment as we pulled into the driveway of our home, especially after a long drive. It was meant to elicit a laugh, or at least a smile, after a long journey, but these days it can be a real accomplishment making it from point A to point B on our frantic highways. And anyone who drove with Ed knew that he was something of a moving hazard himself.

In one sense, "cheating death" is what life is all about. There are hazards everywhere, from birth through the golden years. Those who survive are fortunate.

The popular TV show *Survivor* capitalized on that theme. The survivor was the one who outlasted his or her opponent and walked away with all the money. It was fun and profitable to be the last one left standing.

But in real life, being a survivor is not always great fun. In the 1980 film *Ordinary People*, a teenage boy survived a sailing accident, while his brother drowned. Conrad was guilt-ridden, as if he had done something terribly wrong. The young man was haunted by his memories of the accident, and after attempting suicide, spending time in a mental institution, and undergoing months of therapy, the truth finally came out: he was guilty of surviving! His brother, Buck, had gotten all the accolades for sports and academics, while Conrad had always been just the less accomplished younger brother. Yet it turned out that he was the strong one. The survivor. The one who hung on to the boat.

Every obituary lists survivors. The ones who are hanging on, if only by a thread. If you are reading this book, most likely you are among them. It can be a painful identity, and one that is difficult to embrace. To do so requires you not only to accept loss but also to accept your own strength. You are the strong one. You are the survivor. What are you going to do now?

I have a family portrait hanging in my home. It was taken when Ed and I lived in California with our dog family—Buck, Ramey, and Spike. When I look at that picture, my instant thought is always, *They're all gone.* I'm the only survivor.

When you lose a loved one, especially one with whom you have shared responsibilities, their loss is more than just an emotional one. There are many practical implications as well. Maybe he always changed the oil in your car. Maybe she managed the finances. Now you have to do it. Or have to find a way to get it done! What are your new responsibilities now that you are a survivor? Are you up to the challenge? Maybe you are more ready than you know, though you may feel some resistance. When Ed and I first got married, we divvied up the household tasks. One of his tasks was dusting. In the later years he often slacked off and waited till we were getting company, and then dusted at the last possible moment. Now, even a few years later, and into my second marriage, in which we have a different kind of arrangement, I find myself waiting, as if for Ed to do his dusting chores. Well, I don't like dusting! Why do you think I negotiated that arrangement in the first place?

What are the strengths that you bring to your new responsibilities? Even if you think you can't do it, it may be only that you have not yet flexed those muscles. Maybe you can learn a new skill. You're not used to keeping the checkbook up to date? Try putting it on the computer instead of doing it by hand. In other words, think outside the box. Take note of the other survivors around you. How have they adjusted to their changing life situation?

One day I was outside working on my flowers. I heard the front door open and turned toward it as my husband emerged. In my mind's eye, I saw Ed walking out the door, but the next instant I saw Eric. In my perception, it was surrealistic, almost as if the image of Ed had morphed into Eric. It was all in my head, of course. But every day with Eric I am reminded of both of our losses. His wife, Adrianne; my husband, Ed. How strange it is that from four there are now just two. And we two walking into the future together. That's how it is with survivors. We figure out how to make a new path in the wilderness. We nurture each other in the process.

The key to doing well as a survivor lies in the willingness to move ahead, to find what is often called a "new normal." It's not always easy.

I was intrigued several months ago by a news story about the USS *Intrepid*. The *Intrepid* is a 40,000-ton naval ship that was commissioned for service in World War II. It was then used by NASA as a recovery vessel and again saw action in Vietnam. Then it spent twenty-four years docked at a pier in New York, serving as a sea, air, and space museum. The museum closed October 1, 2006, as the ship was readied for a journey to Bayonne, New Jersey, for repairs and eventually Staten Island, New York, for renovations. The plan was to engage the use of several tugboats to pull the ship from its museum pier and tow it to Bayonne. The tugs' combined 30,000 horsepower was completely ineffectual. The ship would not budge. Simply stated, the ship was stuck in the mud that had accumulated over the space of twenty-four years. It took three weeks of dredging and approximately $3 million to pry the *Intrepid* loose and get the ship on its way.

Many who grieve can understand this stuck-in-the mud feeling. Like the *Intrepid*, it's clear that the past life is over. But grief itself becomes a familiar place—a kind of halfway house, or, like the *Intrepid*, a museum. Grief is a journey, not a destination. But it may feel easier (safer?) to stay put in the mud of grief, instead of moving on. Like the tugboats trying to move the *Intrepid*, our efforts to move ahead seem ponderous.

The summer after Ed died, I was determined to go fishing. Widowhood would not keep me from enjoying the sport (and the place of rest) that Ed and I had so enjoyed together. But I was stuck in a certain way of doing things. When Ed and I went fishing together, we had a system in place that worked for us. We took his pickup, which had a canopy, and loaded the back with all the equipment, clothing, and food we needed, as well as the dogs. In later years, we had to modify that plan because Spike couldn't tolerate the stuffy heat in the back of the truck. So we either took two vehicles—one for Ed and the stuff and one for me and the dogs—or, as we did one year, we borrowed a small open trailer from a friend to accommodate the stuff and pulled it with my car. We had talked about buying a very small utility trailer to make things easier but never got around to it.

When it came around to planning for my solo trip, I kept on the same basic track that Ed and I had been on for many years. I wanted to take all the fishing gear, all the dogs (down to two), and all the food for two weeks of fishing. Even though it was just me, I was planning on taking all the equipment, because Ed's daughter Kim and her family were to join me at the resort, and I wanted to give them some things. I still owned Ed's truck but was not comfortable driving it. Plus, the dogs were spoiled by riding in my air-conditioned car. My Subaru would not hold everything I *needed* to take, so I decided to buy a small enclosed utility trailer. My car was already outfitted with the hitch. I just needed to learn how to drive with a trailer.

First, though, I needed to buy the trailer. I scoured the Internet for what I thought would be simple to find: a tiny pull-behind cart to hold the suitcases and equipment. But to no avail. Finally, I started looking locally and went to a well-known dealer. I went home devastated. The salesman treated me like I was a woman who knew nothing about trailers—which of course I was! But his attitude was unhelpful at best. I stewed for a while and then finally called a few other places and found another place that had an eight-foot enclosed trailer. It was bigger than what I wanted, but it seemed like the smallest thing available. I bought it and asked them to deliver it to my house. That would give me space to learn how to use it. They parked it in my driveway, and I began immediately to learn how to hook it up to my hitch. When I mastered that, I started driving. First, just in and out of the driveway. Backing up felt completely backward to me, and I felt like I was getting nowhere fast, but I kept at it. Then, gradually, I started driving around the block, and then a few blocks away, maneuvering it around in empty parking lots. I was getting better at it, but I still felt uneasy about driving it 200 miles to my fishing resort and back. And my ego still smarted from the experience with the smart-aleck trailer salesman. I had a hunch he was right about me, and that didn't feel good.

But I *had* to go fishing. And I wanted to keep things as normal as I could. But what was normal now? Using the trailer seemed like the next best thing to taking the pickup. The thing I had not yet quite mastered was the art of finding the new normal. One day I was sitting in my car and—I don't remember why—I looked up towing in the manual. It said that my car had a towing limit of 1,000 pounds. Well, the trailer itself weighed more than that! That was it. Time to start dredging up the mud around the stuck vessel. Time to discover a new normal and start moving toward it.

I parked the trailer, and there it sat for several weeks just like the *Intrepid*. Meanwhile I tried to think outside my old box. *Maybe* I could get some kind of a cartop carrier, and *maybe* I could downsize my load. And that's what I did. I got a double soft-sided cartop carrier that I could handle easily by myself. I bought a smaller cooler and decided I could make a few trips to the grocery store. And I told the dogs that they would have to live with a little less space in the back of the car. Then we loaded up and went. All was well. Except I had to decide what to do with the trailer! Ultimately the trailer found a new home. By the time I sold it, I was sad to see it go. It was like saying good-bye to a friend, because through that trailer I had learned an important lesson. I could still go fishing, *and* I could find a new way.

MY TRAVEL JOURNAL

1. How do you feel about being a survivor?
2. What skills or gifts have you begun to discover?
3. What keeps you from fully engaging with life?

SUGGESTED ITINERARY

Write up an *"Intrepid"* list. What are some areas where you feel stuck in the mud—but want to move?

Beside each "stuck" point, write down the name of a person or an activity that could help get you unstuck.

Dare to ask for help.

Hope

In the movie *Schindler's List,* there is a very tense moment when Schindler—the German businessman whose creative scheming saved many Jewish lives—stands beside a Nazi officer on the platform of a train station on a sweltering hot day. A train carrying its human cargo stops briefly on its way to the death camp. The people inside the train are suffocating, sticking hands out between cracks and crying for water. Having compassion for the people, Schindler grabs a hose, turns on the water, and sprays it over the top of the train cars, so that the water trickles in on the people inside. The officer stops him. He says, "You should not do that. You will give them hope, and that would be cruel."

Grieving people can often relate to that statement. Can you? Hope does seem cruel at times. You just start feeling a little bit better, a little bit as if life is worth living, when something else happens to dash your hopes against the rocks of despair.

Yet hope is the very substance that sustains us, especially during times of grief and loss.

There's a story about a young student who took a test at school. One of the questions she had to answer was this: "Upon what do hibernating animals subsist during the winter?" The little girl thought for a moment and then wrote: "All winter long, hibernating animals subsist on the hope of a coming spring!" Hope is powerful medicine, isn't it? And as humans we know that hope is mainly what we subsist on. Hope is vital to living a life that has purpose, direction, and health. This is true all the time, but never more so than during times of grief. Grieving, for humans, is much like hibernating is for a bear or the cocoon stage of a butterfly. It may feel and look like nothing is happening, on the outside at least. Yet it is a very active time in the depths of your being, and hope is what sustains the process.

My sailor husband tells novice sailors that there is nothing more important than knowing where the wind is coming from. You can have an expensive boat and all the training you need, but, as he says, "If you don't know which way the wind is blowing, you don't know anything." In times of grief, you need to feel the wind of hope. It would be virtually impossible to navigate the waters of grief if you did not believe that there was something worth finding on the other side. If you do not have hope, you have nothing. On the other hand, if you have hope, you can weather anything.

Hope is the key. But let me be clear about what hope is. Hope is not simply wishful thinking (which is passive), nor is it the same thing as coping (which means adapting). Hope is very active, and it is open to all possibilities. When you hope, you reach out into the future, knowing that God is there waiting for you. Hope does not deny the pain of grief, but it knows that God is good and that the future is bright with possibility. So hope is a lot like faith. The apostle Paul suggests that Christians should "not grieve as others do who have no hope" (1 Thessalonians 4:13). You must grieve because you have sustained a great loss. But you grieve with hope. Hope does not deny that there is a hole in your heart because your loved one is gone. But hope also knows that there is a bigger picture. It allows you to grieve, and it allows you to find a new path in the midst of the wilderness.

So where does one get this wonderful, life-giving commodity? Hope can't be bought or borrowed. It can't be simply conjured up from the depths of your own being. It is directly related to your relationship with God. You have hope *because* of what God has done for you and *because* you have responded in faith. In Jesus Christ, God has reached out in love, and if you have grasped hold of this love, then hope is at your disposal. Hope is a gift from God, given in the context of a loving relationship. But hope isn't necessarily something that you experience easily or instantaneously. Hope is something that is formed in you as you walk with God.

Where to start? Well, the first step in the journey toward hope is called **suffering**. I know that's not where you want to go, and

101

neither do I, but it's where the journey starts. Let me share with you a brief passage from Paul's letter to the Romans that follows directly on the heels of a statement about having peace with God because of our being justified by faith:

> And not only that, but we also boast in our sufferings, knowing that suffering produces endurance, and endurance produces character, and character produces hope, and hope does not disappoint us, because God's love has been poured into our hearts through the Holy Spirit that has been given to us. (Romans 5:3-5)

The word translated "suffering" also means pressure. Now, that has a familiar ring to it, doesn't it? Life is pressing in on us all the time, and notably during times of grief. Inside, many people feel as if they are in a pressure cooker of feelings, struggles, and dilemmas. Suffering is not fun, but it does provide you with an opportunity. In the midst of suffering, you have the opportunity to begin the journey toward hope (which is just another word for Emmaus!).

So suffering, or pressure, is the first step on this journey toward hope. But those who are discerning will recognize that it can also be the first step toward despair. What makes the difference? The journey to hope is not automatic, and it's not the suffering itself that will lead you there. But Jesus will take you there if you keep walking with him *through the struggle*. The problem is that in suffering, it's easy to leave off following Jesus and walk with other things. Anger, bitterness, selfishness, and pride may become your constant companions on the road instead of the love and grace of Jesus. Be sure of this: they will not lead you to the same place that Jesus will! So it is that two people can experience a similar event in their lives yet one will find hope while the other will find despair. The choices you make in the midst of your suffering will make all the difference.

Those who turn to Christ in the midst of suffering begin to experience a thing called *endurance*, or perseverance. This word means literally to "abide under" something. You abide under the suffering. You experience it, you suffer with it, but you are not crushed by it. When I was a kid, my sister Karen and I used to like to walk down a gravel road to where there was a big culvert. This culvert was at the bottom of a hill, and it provided drainage for that road during heavy rains. It was about five or six feet in diameter, so we had no trouble standing up and playing in it. The best fun was when a car would come by, which didn't happen terribly often on that remote road, but when it did we used to laugh about being run over by a car, and not a scratch on us. Another picture that might be helpful is walking in a rainstorm. The wind is blowing; the rain is beating down. You don't have an umbrella, but Jesus does, so you walk next to him. You abide in Jesus under the circumstances of your life.

When you hang in there under Jesus' umbrella, the experience of suffering changes you. You begin to develop *character*. The idea conveyed by the word *character* is that someone has been approved after going through a trial. You might think of Olympic hopefuls going through the various meets that determine their relative readiness to compete in the Olympics. Or you might think about how gold or silver or other precious metals are refined through fire. The fire purges all of the metal's impurities, and when it is done, the metal is pure. And there is another interesting point to be made. I recently learned how a refiner knows when the refining process is complete. It's when the refiner can see his reflection in the molten metal—because then all the impurities are gone. So it is for you. The job is not done until God's reflection can be seen in you. That's character.

Character, in turn, produces *hope*, the hope that will not disappoint. In the New Testament, hope is synonymous with confidence. You can have confidence when suffering has helped you to endure and has created character in you. It's not confidence in your own strength or confidence that everything will turn out the way you want it to, though.

This hope is not situation-based, and that's the magic of it. The reason this hope does not disappoint us is "because God's love has been poured into our hearts through the Holy Spirit that has been given to us." So, you can have hope, *no matter what!*

MY TRAVEL JOURNAL

1. Is hope a part of your life? How do you experience that reality?

2. What do you still need?

SUGGESTED ITINERARY

In honor of your loved one,

- plant a tree
- volunteer at a soup kitchen
- send a contribution to his or her favorite charity

Are We There Yet?

Have you ever been driving on a familiar road and, when you reach your destination or turnoff, suddenly realize that you had "spaced out" the details of the trip? You have arrived, but you don't remember the scenery or the other cars or even the road signs? How did you get there?

Grief is like that. There is sometimes a slight sense of disorientation, as if you have stepped off the space-time continuum. As I write these words, it has been over three and a half years since Ed died. How can that be? I can still see him sitting in his chair the day he died, staring into space. Still hear his laugh. Still hear the doctor say, "The fight is over."

A friend of mine has been widowed for over six years. She told me that it still feels like her husband is just in the next room. He is still so real, so alive in her memory. That's true for me, too. I can't think of Ed as being dead (that is, inanimate). I can only think of him in life.

Yet, when I look back on the road, so much has happened. When I list it all, it's dizzying. It almost feels like being in a time warp at times. Once in a while it still happens that someone will call and ask for Ed. Usually it's someone he had counseled in the past, someone who somehow missed hearing about what happened to him. I always hesitate before I am able to give a cogent response. It's easier now to say, "Ed died," than it was at first. But the words still catch in my throat.

How long does it take to get better? How long before life becomes normal again? Good questions, but there's no universal answer. For many people, going through all the seasons of a year helps them to come out at the other end feeling ready to face the realities of life. But it's not true for everybody. I've noticed, for instance, that people who lose a spouse often take much longer to reach Emmaus if the marriage was struggling. People expect it to be otherwise and are often surprised that it takes the grieving person so long, but one problem with grief is that we don't just mourn what we had. We also mourn the things we never had. So the grieving spouse who had a bad marriage has a double grief to contend with. Parents who lose a child have to contend with the deep loss and sense of disorientation that comes with an event that is out of sync with the normal flow of events. Children are not supposed to die before their parents. It also makes a difference what the circumstances were surrounding the death itself. The more traumatic the death, the longer it may take to recover. On the other hand, if the death has occurred after a long illness, there may have been a great deal of grieving going on before the death itself, which may actually shorten the grieving period. It's also true that men and women often deal with their grief differently. Men are more likely to move on more quickly than women. It's not *always* successful, but it often is because many men have the ability to compartmentalize their grief in a way that enables them to cope with both their grief and with a new direction.

I was talking to Michael, a colleague of mine, recently and was somewhat bemoaning a task I had ahead of me. We were (finally) moving into our new church building. It had been a very long haul, worshiping in borrowed space and renting a small house as our ministry center for more than a decade. The task that seemed overwhelming at the moment was the sorting, packing, and moving from the ministry center into our new building. But there was more to it than the physical move. Ed's office. After Ed died, no one moved into his office, so we did not make a lot of changes to it. We used it for a variety of things but left the books and many of Ed's other things intact. When I needed one of his books, I would walk down the hall and get it, and then I would return it since my bookshelves were already full. With the move looming, the sorting had to begin; what to throw away, what to give away, what to move into my new space in the new building. I shared the emotional burden of it with Michael, and as we talked, I began to feel that choking sensation in my throat. Michael picked up on it immediately. "We grieve piecemeal," he said simply. He's right. It doesn't happen all at once, and it doesn't happen in a straight line. If it did, you could tick off the miles like you do in a car. As it is, you may at times lurch uncomfortably from place to place and feeling to feeling.

I think the point to be made is that each person's story is unique, and each person's span of grief is also unique. Don't buy into other people's time schedules or rules. Walk your own road, and do it with the intent of pursuing healing and God's good future. Are we there yet? Well, perhaps the answer to that question is another question: Where is *there*? The Emmaus of your grief journey is not a place on the map. Neither is it a static emotional state. It's the place where you recognize and embrace God's work in your life.

MY TRAVEL JOURNAL

1. How long have you been on the road to Emmaus? How do you feel about that?

2. Where is God at work in your life?

SUGGESTED ITINERARY

Create an Emmaus time line. Include whatever events you consider significant, with an arrow marking "I am here." Note where Emmaus is, relative to where you are today.

Talk to God about your journey.

Reconnecting

When I am driving home, I usually have several different roads that I can take. If it's a north-south trip, I most often choose the Garden State Parkway. The entrance is close to my home, and the Parkway is often the most direct route. But sometimes the Parkway turns into a parking lot. At other times it is simply overcrowded, and it feels better to take one of the back roads. When that happens, I exit early and take a road that parallels the Parkway instead. It's more scenic, less traffic, and somewhat less likely to become a stop-and-go situation. When I exit onto Double Trouble Road (so named because it leads to a park by the same name), I can, for a time, watch the traffic whizzing by (or not!) on the Parkway that is within easy view. Meanwhile I am in my own parallel universe, driving along in a more comfortable setting.

The road to Emmaus can often feel like being in a parallel universe. You are driving along on your road of grief, taking your sweet time, while the rest of the world races by at its own frantic pace.

Sometimes it may even feel like you are leading a double life. There's work to be done, bills to be paid, family gatherings to be attending, kids to be cared for, errands to run. On the surface you try to keep your chin up, put on a happy face, and pretend that you are back in the swim. People may even observe that you are doing great; you are back involved in life. Yet on the inside, and in your private moments, you are still struggling along on the Emmaus road.

This double life is due, in part, to the culture we live in. People who are grieving often find that there is little support for their emotional journey. Those around you simply want you to feel better and get back to normal without bringing the rest of the group down. Our society is not big on grief, even though loss is a normal daily experience. It's as if people believe that denying its existence will make it go away (or not come *their* way!). So those who grieve are often forced off the road, so to speak, to deal with their feelings alone.

Another reality is that you simply need time to heal, and you may need to retreat from normal activities for a time in order to do that. If you can't take a leave of absence from your normal duties, you may have to deal with your grief in doses at those times when you can leave the main road and take the scenic route instead.

Either way, there will come a time when you feel the need to integrate your two lives—to bring Emmaus and your previous life together somehow. Just remember, the goal is not simply to return to normal, but to find a *new* normal.

A part of the reconnecting process involves your social contacts. You may no longer have the same motivation for continuing certain activities or relationships. Or, you may find that some people who were friends before don't call anymore. On the other hand, you may suddenly find that there are people out there whom you had not noticed before and activities that now sound appealing. Perhaps it's time to initiate some new things. Invite people to your home, or suggest meeting for coffee at a restaurant. Take up square dancing!

If the person you lost was your spouse, you may contemplate dating and possibly another marriage. And if you do get married again, what then? Here's what I've learned. If you marry someone who is not afraid of her or his own feelings and who is willing to cry with you, then you don't have to be afraid of bringing your memories with you. Of course it is possible to be so overburdened with grief that you can't fully give yourself to another person. If that's the case, then you're not ready to invest yourself in that new relationship! (In other words, don't use a new relationship as a "fix" when what you need is healing.) When you are grieving, there is a sense in which you are still "in relationship" with your former spouse, and that can get in the way of establishing a second lasting relationship. You need to get to a certain point of recovery before making that second commitment. There's an old rule of thumb that you need to wait a year before making any serious new commitments (whether that new commitment is a relationship or a financial investment, a new job or a move), but only you can know when the time is right to move ahead. Let God guide you in this, as in all things, and trust the wisdom that God gives.

Often the process of reconnecting requires some tough emotional work. Early on in your grief, for instance, when you first recognized your anger or other hard feelings, they may have seemed too overwhelming to address. But now that you've experienced God's grace along the way, you may have sufficient strength to approach some of those challenging tasks—forgiveness, for instance. Is there someone you need to forgive? Is it the person who died or the doctors who in their humanness could not save him or God who seemed oblivious to your pleas or maybe yourself?

Lewis Smedes says that God did not give us the power to change the past, only to remember it. He explains: "This would be no great problem if the past had not saddled us with wrongs that people have done us, wrongs we can neither undo nor forget, wrongs that infest our memories and make us sick. Once we are wounded and wronged, the gift of memory becomes an inability to forget. And our inability to forget becomes our inability to be glad about life. . . . We are discovering that the only way to get over the misery of resentment for remembered wrongs is to forgive the people who did them."

When we forgive, Smedes says, "we set a prisoner free and then discover that the prisoner we set free was us." He outlines a process of four steps toward the grace of forgiveness:

1. We hurt.
2. We hate.
3. We heal ourselves.
4. We come together.

That last stage, the coming together, is not always possible (especially if the person has died!). But it is still possible to achieve the healing grace of forgiveness even if reconciliation is not feasible. [1]

I hope it's clear, looking at Smedes's process, that forgiveness is no quick fix. It is a tough road to walk—one that rivals the

Emmaus road in difficulty, but one that also rivals the Emmaus road in its profound healing properties.

In her book *Left to Tell*, Immaculée Ilibagiza tells the horrific experience of living through the Rwandan holocaust in 1994. She survived along with several other women who were hidden for months in a bathroom. Most of the rest of her family (and many friends) were brutally killed. When Immaculée left her hiding place and re-entered society, she gradually discovered the details of her parents' and siblings' deaths. Because of her Christian faith, she wanted to forgive the perpetrators of these crimes. But she was hounded (understandably) by feelings of anger, rage, and desire for revenge.

Here's how she describes her feelings when she finally was able to forgive: "A sudden rush of air flooded my lungs. I heaved a heavy sigh of relief, and my head dropped back on the pillow. I was at peace again. Yes, I was sad—deeply sad—but my sadness felt good. I let it embrace me and found that it was clean, with no tinge of bitterness or hatred. I missed my family desperately, but the anger that had gripped me like a returning malignancy was gone."[2]

In your reconnecting, don't forget the One whom you have met along the way. The healing grace that you experienced on the road is not just for you to *feel better*. Emmaus is all about meeting God and understanding that God is involved in your life, no matter what! Once you've been to Emmaus, you can't be the same again. You will re-enter life, but it will be with a new understanding and a new sense of what life is all about. And that will give you a new direction and purpose. God's purpose.

When the two disciples recognized Jesus in their dining room in Emmaus, they immediately hightailed it back to Jerusalem. Emmaus was their turning point, but it was not the destination! Emmaus pointed them back into life. What came next was a new adventure that would turn out to be even more astounding than the adventure they had already experienced with Jesus.

What's next for you? What new direction will you go once you've been to Emmaus?

MY TRAVEL JOURNAL

1. Talk to God about the person you need to forgive.

2. Where have you begun to reconnect with life? What help do you still need?

SUGGESTED ITINERARY

Make that phone call you've been putting off.

Notes

1. Lewis Smedes, *Forgive and Forget* (San Francisco: Harper Collins Publishers, 1996), x–xi.

2. Immaculée Ilibagiza, *Left to Tell* (Carlsbad, CA: Hag House, Inc., 2006), 197.

Elaine's Story

"I can't help but think I should be in a different place by now,"
Elaine said to me recently. It's been more than five years since her
husband, Dan, died. They had been married just short of forty-five
years. "I figured that by a year after Dan died, I would be in a simple ranch house, maybe in a retirement village with a pool."
Instead, she is still in the Cape Cod house that she and Dan had
shared for many years, surrounded by clutter. Her desire to be in
"a different place" is a reference to her emotional life as well as
her geographic location. She sees the clutter as an outward mani-
festation of a turbulent inner life that stretches back over a period
of years, long before Dan's death. Now she feels as if she can't
move ahead until the clutter is gone.

Her marriage to Dan was not the stuff of fairy tales, though,
when she met him, she thought he could walk on water. She was
just eighteen, working in the local sweet shop where everyone
stopped for a snack. Dan was twenty-nine, a budding journalist
for the local newspaper. They came from radically different back-
grounds. He came from a moneyed family in Pennsylvania—his
parents lost their fortune in the 1929 stock market crash. She was
from a working-class family in New Jersey. Dan's family life was
genteel and quiet on the surface, yet an undercurrent of turbulence
was revealed when his parents separated. Elaine's mother was
quiet and circumspect, but her father was very communicative.

Dan and Elaine were so different, and yet they were "blown
together" she says, "by a strange wind. In some sick way we needed
each other."

"I married my mother," Elaine says now. Like her mother,
Dan was gentle and kind. But painfully quiet. "His silence was
deafening," she says. More than anything, she wanted him to
talk, to be involved with her and with family decisions. But he

wouldn't . . . couldn't. He didn't seem to have that same need. "I never had a soul mate," she says regretfully.

Elaine met Dan just a few months before her mother died. She now believes that grief over her mother's death, coupled with her own young age, made her vulnerable to jumping into a relationship that was not the fairy tale she had envisioned. She and Dan did all the things that married people do: had two kids, traveled, took care of the household, and created an extended circle of mutual friends. They developed mutual interests, in particular antiquing. But there was always something missing. As the years went by, Elaine became more and more upset and angry.

They went to counseling several times in their nearly forty-five years of marriage. He didn't resist going but would always back away from it in the end. "I'm not going back," he said finally, and that was it. They established something of a truce that lasted until Dan died on February 1, 2002.

Dan's death was a shock to Elaine. In spite of the fact that he was eleven years older, she expected to go first because her parents had died at much younger ages than his had (her mother was fifty-two and her father was sixty-three). One day Dan developed a terrible abdominal pain that was quickly diagnosed as advanced liver cancer. The oncologist was less than encouraging (and none too kind, Elaine remembers). Dan came away from the appointment "feeling like a goner." He thought it was all over for him, but he agreed to go to an appointment at a well-known cancer clinic. About a week before that appointment, he was sitting at the kitchen table, testing his blood sugar (he had been a diabetic for a few years). "I am so tired," he had said earlier. Suddenly Elaine noticed that he was not acting right; then he slumped over and laid his head down on the table. She called 911, telling them that it was a diabetic attack. The first-aid squad members who came quickly saw that it was something else—a stroke—and they rushed him to the local hospital. He was in the hospital for less than two weeks, and in the meantime had a second stroke that put him in a coma. Elaine and her close family members took shifts sitting with him. The night before he died, Elaine spoke to him, and though she knew he could not respond, she explained that she had signed a living will on his behalf, told him that she loved him and that she would see that everything was taken care of—and that she would be okay. He died with his son and daughter, Chris and Lisa, at his side. That seemed appropriate to Elaine, given the nature of their marriage.

Tears have not been a big part of Elaine's grief. "And I can cry at the drop of a hat." Instead, after Dan died, Elaine went on autopilot. "Just doing what I had to do," she said. There was, however, "a big hole in my gut." And that hole refused to budge. She felt as if it would be there forever, haunting her. But there were other feelings, too. Mainly anger. "He left me in a way that he didn't have to talk," Elaine says ruefully about the stroke that left him comatose.

So, she was left with anger. And regret. She felt the loss of the relationship, and she felt intense grief over the relationship she had hoped she would have—and didn't. She also regretted that she did not come to the point of accepting him for who he was before he died. Now, when she plays a CD of Puccini's music that he and she both loved, she gets emotional because there was always a point in the music when Dan would get her attention and make sure she heard it. "That was how he communicated his feelings," she said, "but I couldn't understand it."

On the first Christmas without Dan, Elaine decided to go on a cruise in order to be away from the memories. What she discovered was that the memories followed her onto the cruise ship. Now, she says, she is working on reinventing Christmas. Much of that reinvention involves her faith. The place she wants to be on Christmas Eve is at church.

At first she pulled away from church, though. The idea of walking into a roomful of people was just too overwhelming to her. "I thought I'd bawl," she recalls, "but I need God in my life." So she started attending Saturday evening service, which was a much smaller, more intimate setting. Plus, Elaine is not a morning person, so Saturday evening became her worship service. It fit her.

A few months after Dan died, a friend suggested that she attend a grief group, which came to be known as the "good grief" group.

It was late May when she joined the group, and that became a major source of support and healing for her. Finally, she found a forum for her pain to be expressed. Finally, she found a group where she didn't need to explain herself. She could just be. Many of the people in that group became friends for life. After the group disbanded formally, the members continued to gather, and even today, some of them get together for lunch and conversation.

"All of a sudden one day," she said, after getting back to church, and after being a part of the grief recovery group, the hole in her heart seemed to fill up a bit. And she started to feel better, to become engaged with life again. Elaine still struggles with many feelings: regret, anger, and deep grief. But along the way she has begun to discover that the God whom she so needs in her life is also the one who can fill the deep hole she has in her heart.

She finds encouragement from a quote by Aeschylus that she chanced to hear on the radio: "He who learns must suffer. And even in our sleep pain that cannot forget falls drop by drop upon the heart, and in our own despair, against our will, comes wisdom to us by the awful grace of God."

MY TRAVEL JOURNAL

1. What part of Elaine's story do you relate to?

2. If you were Elaine's friend, what would you do to support her on her journey?

SUGGESTED ITINERARY

Listen to some good music.

Go somewhere that you can walk barefoot—in the sand, in the grass—and breathe fresh air. Feel the earth under your feet and the breeze on your skin.

PART FIVE

Return to Emmaus

Emmaus Revisited

I woke up on a Sunday morning a few years back, ready to tackle my usual Sunday duties. But in the midst of my stretching exercises, I was laid flat by an attack of vertigo that made me feel incredibly seasick. For a few weeks I had experienced minor episodes of vertigo, waves of dizziness that would wash over me when I turned over in bed, and then would quickly subside. It reminded me of how I used to feel as a kid riding carnival rides. Then it was a "fun" dizzy. But no more. This was serious stuff. I could barely walk, and when I did I ran into walls. Preaching was out of the question that day, as was driving. Since Ed was preaching elsewhere that day, I was up the proverbial creek. I called Candy, my usual substitute, and she agreed to preach my sermon for me. The next day I dizzily made a visit to my regular doctor, who gave me some medicine to stabilize my vertigo, then sent me to an ear, nose, and throat specialist. He diagnosed the condition as *benign positional vertigo*. Certain crystals in my inner ear had become dislodged and were sending wrong signals to my brain. There was a fix that included turning me abruptly upside down, and then right side up again—sort of a snow globe effect. Then I had to stay upright for several days. It worked. When I went back, he said I was cured. "But," he added, "that doesn't mean it won't happen again." He explained that it was like getting over a cold—you can get another one. "If you bump your head again" (that was the supposed cause), "you could knock the crystals loose again." Sure enough, it *has* happened again; though my subsequent bouts have been much milder.

If you take a journey to Emmaus, you may want to believe that once you have gone there, you'll never journey there again. But that is far from true. Loss is a constant in life. You will return. Perhaps your next journey will be brief. Or maybe it will be a lengthy stay. But you will be back, so be prepared.

Surely you've noticed that some places you visit stay in your heart. Emmaus is like that, in a bittersweet kind of way. That's not such a bad thing, though. Remember, the road to Emmaus is God's gift. It's the way to healing and hope. Don't be afraid to return to Emmaus. Good things happen there.

I've returned to Emmaus a few times myself. Here are three of my stories.

Brenda

My relationship with Brenda began just a week before Ed died. Very quickly she became a close confidant and friend. Her husband, Bill, had already been my friend for a while, and that relationship deepened as he drew close to Ed and me in Ed's illness, and later was the pastor to officiate at Ed's memorial. Brenda's ministry was even more personal than that. Because she had lost her first husband to lung cancer, she knew about my particular grief. She was among the few who could tell stories that hit incredibly close to home for me. So, she walked with me on my journey. But she was on a journey as well, so I became a companion to her too.

Some thirty years earlier, Brenda had Hodgkin's disease, which was cured through radiation therapy. Her experience was remarkably like the experience of Eric's wife, Adrianne. At the time the radiation was a new, lifesaving therapy. Prior to that time, patients with Hodgkin's would only live a couple of years at the most. But with the new radiation therapy, patients were beginning to survive and thrive for many years. But the radiation had a dark side. The total-body radiation caused side effects that, for most patients, emerged many years later. Nerve damage and damage to heart and lung muscle, even additional cancers, were sometimes blamed on the radiation. Brenda's primary result was cardiovascular, with implications for the lung function as well as breast cancer. When I began to understand Brenda's physical situation, one of the first things I did was invite Brenda and Bill and Eric and Adrianne for dinner so they could meet. Adrianne and Brenda were both amazed to find each other because the similarities were so striking, and each had thought she was alone. Both had a very fragile look about them physically, but both were very strong emotionally and mentally. Though they had very different personalities, they were both fighters.

When Adrianne died in 2005, I wondered inwardly how long Brenda would survive. She lived another year and a half. She fought hard, but progressively became weaker.

In the summer of 2006, Brenda and Bill lost their golden retriever, Knox. By the end of September, Brenda was gone too. Bill gave me a picture of Brenda and Knox by the ocean, and we used it for the cover of the memorial service program. I couldn't help but think that it was a great picture of what heaven must be like.

Brenda spent a few weeks in the University of Pennsylvania Hospital, and that's where she died. Because of the distance, I only got to see her once while she was there, though she and I talked several times by phone. On one of those occasions, she candidly talked to me about her impending death. She was under no illusions that she would get well. She was ready to go, she said, though she worried about Bill and about her son Matt who, although he was an adult, still had a lot of growing up to do.

Brenda gave me gifts in both her living and her dying. In her life, she gave me strength for my own difficult journey. In her dying, she gave me a model of candor and acceptance. It was about a week after Brenda died that Katie (Bill's daughter) discovered a little scrap of paper in Brenda's purse. On the paper was a quotation from Robert Louis Stevenson: "Life is not a matter of holding good cards, but of playing a bad hand well."

Doing Brenda's memorial was a revisit to the Emmaus road for me. I poured my heart into every aspect of the work. When I was done, I was completely drained. I still miss her, but I will always treasure the gifts she gave me.

Bob

My friend Teddy called me late one night, a couple of months after Brenda died, with a need that I recognized instantly. Her husband's life was slipping away, and she wasn't sure where to turn. His kidney cancer had spread into other organs, including the brain, and finally he was just not himself. She was having a crisis that night in knowing how to care for him, and she called me. I knew instinctively why Teddy had called *me*. She didn't call for medical advice, because I had none to give. And she didn't call so that I would come over to help—I was 3,000 miles away! Bob and Teddy were in Oregon, and I was in New Jersey. But she knew that she was on a road that I had traveled, so she called me. And I listened. Then I gave her the best advice I could and told her I would pray for her and for Bob. A day later, he was in a hospice care facility, and a few days after that, he was gone.

Though I was far away, I felt the loss deeply. Teddy is a person with a very tender heart, and I knew that her love for Bob was deep. Plus, Teddy had been such a good friend to both Ed and me when we lived in Oregon. Our friendship had already spanned the distance of time and geography. And both Teddy and Bob had met Eric and had given their thumbs-up to our marriage. I had hoped for other visits back to Oregon to see both Teddy and Bob.

I felt inundated with death. Enough. Every death takes me back to Emmaus! I don't want to go there anymore! And yet, I know I must.

Misty and Me

There's a popular book called *Marley and Me* by John Grogan in which the author chronicles the poignant relationship between human and dog. Marley was a yellow Labrador retriever whose antics bring both laughter and tears to the reader.

Misty was also a yellow Lab. She was the dog I didn't want, but who became a soul mate of sorts. Misty came to us in the fall of 1998, just a couple of months after we lost Buck (also a yellow Lab). When Buck died, Ed and I were both devastated. But we handled our grief somewhat differently. He immediately wanted to get another dog (never mind that we still had Ramey and Spike—Buck had been his hunting buddy and was his best dog friend). I was not opposed to another dog, but I wanted some time to grieve first. For him, looking up Labradors on the Internet was a way of coping, and I finally gave in. He found a litter of pups that seemed to have just what he wanted (which was a clone of Buck—a yellow male). The breeder was near the upper Delaware River where we spent our annual fishing vacation, so we planned to pick up the puppy while we were there in September. But then some things went awry. The mom had trouble with her litter; she only had four to begin with (a small litter for Labs) and then lost two by sleeping on them. The only pups left were a black male and a yellow female. Since we still had our two black Labs, we opted for the yellow female.

While we were at the river observing the typical misty mornings, we came up with the name *Misty Morning Surprise* for our new puppy. She *was* a surprise, since we had planned on a male. I loved Misty, but Ed and that puppy developed a bond that was instant and deep. She was his dog for sure and "just what the doctor ordered" in terms of his grief. He had thought that a clone of Buck was what he needed, but Misty was good medicine for him. It didn't matter that she never became the retriever that Buck had been. She was his new best dog friend, and she remained that friend until the day he died.

Misty was five and a half years old when Ed died. In that space of time, our dog family had transitioned. We lost Ramey at the ripe old age of thirteen and then welcomed Grace. Spike—my best dog buddy—died just a couple of weeks after Ed did, just shy of fourteen. It seemed ironic at the time that my dog went with Ed, and Ed's dog stayed with me. As I thought about it, there seemed to be a good news aspect to that scenario. I was now left with two relatively young dogs. Grace was just two and Misty was five and a half. So I shouldn't have to face any dog losses anytime soon.

Think again. Misty was just over seven when she was diagnosed with lymphoma. She had manifested signs of this disease for months, starting with some blood work that was a little off kilter. Then when I took her for her annual exam in the fall, I asked the vet to examine her closely. He found all of her peripheral lymph nodes enlarged. He told me that lymphoma was a likely diagnosis. But he also asked me a rather pointed question: "What will you do if Misty has cancer? Do you want to put her through chemotherapy?" My answer was instant. *"No, I don't."* The memory of being with Ed through chemotherapy was still too fresh, and I didn't want to put Misty through anything that would just make her sicker (which was my view of chemotherapy at the time). My local vet did not push me to go further with diagnostic tests, and I chose to just wait and see how she would do. The thing was that she seemed healthy, except for those enlarged nodes.

By then, Eric and I were dating, and it seemed tragically ironic that Misty might have lymphoma, just like Adrianne!

Misty stayed healthy until mid-December, when all of a sudden she got a very large swelling under her chin. It was on a Sunday, of course. After church, Eric and I took her to the emergency vet hospital, where both Buck and Spike had died, and where Spike and Misty had both had surgery. The preliminary diagnosis was indeed lymphoma, and after a couple of days, the cytology report confirmed that diagnosis. By that time her face was greatly distorted from the swelling. So I was back to making a decision: treat her or let her go. The doctors there strongly recommended chemotherapy and told me that Misty could conceivably be in remission for a year to a year and a half. At that point, in spite of my reluctance to do chemo, it only seemed fair to Misty to give it a try, and it was nothing short of miraculous to see the cancer literally melt into remission after her first treatment. The first day of her chemo, her neck began to dramatically reduce in size. And I had my dog back. For the next fourteen months, Misty and I went back and forth to her oncologist for chemotherapy and checkups. She went into remission immediately, and the cancer stayed away almost a year. When it reappeared, she went back into chemotherapy and had two more good months. Then suddenly it was clear that the cancer had returned with a vengeance, and there was no turning it back.

During those fourteen months of chemotherapy, Misty was like a new dog. She was playful again (I hadn't realized she had lost her playful energy; I just thought she grew up!), and she even played with Grace from time to time. Going through chemo with Misty was in a sense a healing time for me, because it gave me a chance to see that sometimes chemo works. It also gave me the chance to bond with Misty in a way that we had not bonded before. She and I were family, and we both appreciated that, but in those fourteen months, she became my dog.

Then came the day that I had to give her back to Ed.

Let me tell you about a dream that I had. This dream came just a few weeks after Ed died, but it stayed with me. In the dream, I was carrying Buck through a hospital-like building, filled with sick people. Buck was very sickly and did not look like himself. Somehow (in ways that only work in the dream world), we moved from the second-floor window, down to the front lawn of the place. Ed was there, but I had the distinct impression that I could not go to him. There was an invisible boundary. Ed looked well, healthy, happy. Smiling. Much in contrast to the sick dog in my arms. I walked toward him and did the natural thing. I handed him the dog, and as soon as Buck was in Ed's arms, he bounded off into the distance, healthy and happy.

At the time, I interpreted that dream in terms of my grief. I was handing my grief over to Ed. When Misty was going through chemotherapy, though, and I thought of that dream, Buck morphed into Misty. And the day came when I handed Misty over to Ed: March 2, 2007.

My grief over losing Misty had multiple facets because she was Ed's dog and because I had relived the chemotherapy experience with her—and because we had become so close in those fourteen months. An unexpected sidelight to that loss was that I even began to miss going to the emergency hospital and seeing the people who worked there. Our trips there had been pleasant bonding times for us, and I never begrudged the time or the effort. She liked it too, which said a lot for Misty. She was not your usual gregarious "I love everyone" Labrador. She was choosy about her friends, and those people were most certainly her friends.

There were some striking parallels between the experiences with Misty and with Ed. That was especially noticeable in the last week of life. Death seemed to come so abruptly. Sure, I knew for fourteen months that I would lose Misty. I knew for a year and a half that Ed had lung cancer and could die from it. But the end came so quickly. And then they were gone. In their deaths, each produced a quiet that was palpable. Misty was a high-maintenance dog, and not just because of the trips to the vet. She was neurotic, especially about hard floors. I had to keep rugs everywhere so she could walk from room to room. And she was demanding. Grace never had to beg for food or treats. Misty handled that. Grace never had to bark (except when it was *absolutely necessary*). Misty took care of that. Misty was quite verbal, and she was expressive in other ways as well. She and Eric had a game they played; he calls it the "quiet motel voice." He was trying to get her to learn to talk quietly. She thought it was funny to bark her head off for a while and then grin while she gave a low guttural growl (the motel voice). When she was gone, the house was, as they say, "quiet as a tomb." So we all suffered in that silence.

I was rereading the Emmaus story this morning and was struck by Luke's comment about the two disciples on the road. The stranger has just asked them what they've been talking about on the road, and Luke says, "They stood still, looking sad." When you have lost someone that you love, sometimes that's all you can do.

The sadness in losing Misty has been profound. So has the transformation. The parallel to my first trip to Emmaus has been quite amazing. I thought I would want another dog immediately, and a part of me did. But I decided that it was not the best choice—not right away. Better to try and find out what life would be like with just Grace.

Grace, who had always been the bad dog, rather quickly became much more mellow and manageable. She also started being allowed to go with us almost everywhere. Because of her gregarious and adventurous nature, she was comfortable almost anywhere (contrary to Misty, who was neurotic and did not really like new things all that much). Grace also began to develop a social life apart from us. Eric's son Rick would call up and ask if he could pick Gracie up to go swimming. Off she would go with Rick, his wife, and two young children. Or Eric would take Grace with him to his sailboat. Grace was in heaven. So sometimes

Grace would be home when I got there, sometimes not. I had the freedom to stay late at work or to come home and work in the garden. I didn't have to be there for the dogs.

Misty had needed me. Grace loves me, but she has a life of her own! I miss the dependence and have found it difficult to let that go. But Misty's passing has caused me to transition to a new way of being. It's a kind of freedom, one that is initially tough to accept, but that becomes a new lifestyle.

So, have *you* been back to Emmaus?

People speak of grief recovery, but don't be misled into thinking that you'll simply be "over it." The loss is permanent, and so are the wounds. You'll have a hole in your heart that won't go away. Every new loss will in some way be a reminder of the original loss.

As time goes by, you *will* feel better. Much better. You will laugh again, dance again, live again, love again. But Emmaus will always be a part of your life.

MY TRAVEL JOURNAL

1. When have you returned to Emmaus?
2. What was the experience like?

SUGGESTED ITINERARY

Think about a favorite place where you love to go. Make plans to go there.

Michelle's Story

"My relationship with my mother started at age seven," Michelle says, and that beginning also heralded her first significant loss. Up until that time, she had stayed weekdays with a babysitter whom she called "Grandma Bertha" while her pediatrician single mother, Natalie, was at work. On the weekends she was home with her mom. Michelle recalls those first seven years with great fondness because Grandma Bertha was a wonderful nurturing person, and she gave Michelle a great deal of love. But when Michelle was seven, her mother (for reasons she never quite understood) removed her from Grandma Bertha's home, and from then on Michelle was a latchkey kid. She was devastated because her mom practically forbade contact with Grandma Bertha and her family from that time.

Until Natalie's death, Michelle lived her life in response to that event, and in reaction to her mother, who quite in contrast to Bertha was a controlling and difficult person to live with. The relationship was a difficult one, right up to the end.

Natalie was a tough disciplinarian whose corrections were harsh and, in Michelle's words, "spirit breaking." Michelle's goal as a young person was to keep the peace, so she worked hard to be an obedient daughter. She wasn't always successful. On one occasion, when Michelle was playing with hairspray and matches (admittedly a no-no!) with her friend Bernie, Natalie flew into a rage and vowed that Bernie (who was Grandma Bertha's grandson) would never be allowed in the house again. Often when Natalie was giving one of her famous parties, she would blow off steam at Michelle's expense if her daughter was not getting the housecleaning done as quickly or as well as expected. On one occasion, she got a board out of the garage as a spanking tool. Still, she would demand, "Where's my kiss?" And Michelle would feel compelled to kiss her, though she did not feel much love toward her mother. "On some level I loved her," she says now; "you're supposed to love your mother." She quickly learned not to make waves, and carried that coping mechanism (along with buried anger) into her marriage.

When Natalie was eighty-one, she was diagnosed with dementia. Because Michelle is an only child, the decisions about her mother's care were largely up to her. However, a rather large extended family often entered into the decision-making regarding Natalie's care. Their Filipino culture gave them a preference for home care rather than a nursing home. The idea of a nursing home seemed shameful to them, as if they were sending their sister into exile. The problem was that Natalie's dementia didn't just make her forgetful. She became combative and at times violent. What complicated this situation for Michelle was the problem of distance. Natalie lived in Southern California, in the home where Michelle grew up. Michelle lived in New Jersey.

When Natalie was placed in the hospital and diagnosed with end-stage dementia, Michelle was also making significant changes in her personal life. Her husband had asked for a divorce. Both of her kids had grown up and left home. She decided that she wanted out of the business that she and her husband shared. She also wanted to resolve some of her lifelong issues with her mother. So she went to Southern California to be with her mother who was in the process of dying. Michelle had been reading up on death and dying, and she understood that many people who are dying try to resolve relationships. She had high hopes that her mother would be one of those people. Natalie was not. Instead, she followed the truism that says, "People die as they lived." Natalie kept the walls up, right to the end. Still, Michelle worked hard to make Natalie's passage as positive as it could be. She stayed by her mother's side for two months, hoping and praying that they would have some resolution, some significant change, in the relationship. There was not.

The moment of death was quiet. Many of Natalie's extended family members were at her side, along with Michelle. She was not breathing well, and Michelle tried to comfort her by stroking her forehead and telling her, "It's okay to go." After a time, Natalie stopped breathing. At that moment, Michelle felt helpless. "Even though you know it's coming," she said, "you don't want it to." Helplessness gave way to the practical aspects of funeral preparation and getting ready to go back home. And then came the anger. Anger "because I felt like she gave up. And because she didn't talk to me. I really *really* wanted her to talk to me." A part of the anger was the frustration that Michelle truly wanted to be there for her mom, but she couldn't reach her. Then the lack of resolution "just became one more thing she didn't do for me."

Michelle's grief has gone through a series of major paradigm shifts. She returned home to New Jersey shortly after the funeral and re-entered her own life, which consisted of working her way out of a business relationship with her husband, and then working through the divorce—all the while working as the executor for her mother's estate. Less than a year later she was back in California because her uncle Pepito was dying.

Initially, the management of her mother's estate was a burden, but she has come to see it as a gift, because it means that she does not have to work full-time in order to support herself. Instead of being an owner-operator of her own business, she now works as a client care representative in a veterinarian's office. Though she is overqualified for the job, it has provided a different kind of challenge and a way to transition into a new phase of her life.

Michelle is determined to find healing and to break the pattern of negativity that started between her and her mom (and threatened to continue between Michelle and her two grown children as well). Her determination was symbolized in an event that she held at her home on the date of her mom's birthday, just a little more than a year after Natalie died. The event was a small group worship service focused on commemorating Natalie's death and praying for the healing of Michelle's grief. The choice of that date was very intentional. Her mother's birthday had been a focus of pain since Michelle was a small child when Natalie had accused her of forgetting her mother's birthday and made her come home from Grandma Bertha's, only to subject her to the silent treatment. Michelle never forgot that date again, but it was always a painful remembering, until she decided that it was time to let go of the pain. "Up to that point," Michelle said, "I was trying to rewrite history, to make the relationship better. Finally, I decided that I was going to accept it for what it was. My mom had died, and the relationship was not going to change. But *I* could change." She determined that from that point on, she would take responsibility for herself. So that event became something of a watershed. The pain of the past, if not gone, was greatly diminished. The future seemed brighter. She was no longer angry.

Michelle has been very aware of God's presence with her throughout her process of healing, especially through some special people at her church who became her "Jesus with skin on." Looking back at her time in California while her mother was dying, she realizes that she trusted God to sustain her. Often that sustenance came through phone calls and e-mail from her friends back home in New Jersey. Now her desire is to approach her relationship with God more intentionally. She is working on creating a daily routine of spending time with God, and she is stepping out of her comfort zone by leading a small group study.

Her great desire is to create that spiritual time with God, enjoy a positive relationship with her kids, and spend time with her new granddaughter (named Natalie!).

MY TRAVEL JOURNAL

1. What part of Michelle's story do you relate to?
2. If you were Michelle's friend, what would you do to support her on her journey?

SUGGESTED ITINERARY

Talk to God about the changes in your life. Thank God for helping you through them.

Give yourself a hug.

Again, give yourself a hug.

Plan an event to commemorate where you are in your journey, such as:

- Go out to dinner with a friend.

- Watch a good movie.

- Spend some alone time with just you, God, and your Bible.

Your Story

I didn't see the hummingbirds today.

Just yesterday they were buzzing about my zinnias and lilies, drinking voraciously and dive-bombing each other. Today there are none in sight. No action at the feeder. No hummers attacking each other. Just the finches and chickadees and catbirds going about their business as if nothing had changed. But something has. I surmise that my diminutive friends have begun their journey to a warmer winter climate. Perhaps, if I'm lucky, I will see one or two stragglers before the migration has passed. It's mid-September, and I have been expecting their departure. Every day for the past week, I've snatched as many moments outdoors as possible, watching them, trying for one last photograph. I have known this day would come, as it does every year. I knew I would wake up one day and they would be gone.

Today is the day. But I am no less sad for the knowing of it. They will be back, but I will miss them through the winter months.

As I have been straining my eyes for a glimpse of tiny wings all day, I have also been waiting anxiously for a call from my sister Janet. Mom is in the hospital having some complications following cancer surgery. She is eighty-eight. This, too, feels like a turning point, one that is as inevitable as the migration of the hummingbirds.

So, this is where my story ends, with the continuing cycle of life and the feelings and struggles that go along with it. As long as I am alive, I know that I will experience more losses. I also know from experience that if I continue to embrace my grief in each loss, I will continue to grow and be transformed. My confidence in God is great. My mother and her family are in God's hands, and in the most ultimate and profound sense, all will be well. But there will be more struggles and more grief along the way.

I am reminded today of the story of a little boy who went with his father to the dog pound. While they were there, they met lots of dogs of various sizes and shapes. Finally, the little boy came upon a mixed breed mutt who wagged his tail vigorously when the little boy petted him. "I'll take this one," he said rather decisively.

"Why this one?" his father quizzed him.

"Because I want the one with the happy ending," the boy said.

Isn't that what we all want? The one with the happy ending.

In Jesus that happy ending is assured. That is what enables us to grieve with hope, even when all seems bleak in the terms of this world. In this life, there is no promise of a fairy-tale ending to our struggles. That's where faith comes in. We hope for that which we cannot yet see. We trust that God, who has been faithful in ages past, will be just as faithful in the days to come. One day we will all be home. In the meantime, as each loss comes to us, we walk the Emmaus road and look for help along the way.

All along in this book I have encouraged you to embrace your own story, difficult as it may be. I hope you have been able to do that. Whatever else is true, it's *your* story, unique in itself as you are unique. At the same time, I hope too that you have discovered a kinship with some of the other stories that I have told.

I encourage you now to summarize your experience with grief thus far. Tell your story. Again! If you are working with a support group, tell it to your group. If you are not, find a compassionate friend who will listen to your story. If you like to write, put it down on paper. As you do, listen to yourself. How far have you come? Thank God!

Feel free to use the following questions to guide you in the telling of your story.

MY TRAVEL JOURNAL

1. Describe the loved one who died and what your relationship was like with that person.

2. How did the death occur? What were some of the memorable events surrounding the death?

3. What were some of your feelings early on?

4. What has life been like for you since he or she died? What have been some of the turning points for you since then?

5. When did you start to get better? What helped?

6. Where have you seen God in the process of your healing?

7. Where are you now?

8. What do you still need?

SUGGESTED ITINERARY

When you get done telling your story, just remember, it's not really the end. It's merely a stop along the way. There's much more to come, both losses and gains. Trust God for the journey, and God will surely bring you all the way home.

Companions on the Road to Emmaus

A Grief Support Group

Facilitator's guide online at www.judsonpress.com

Participant's Guide

Companions on the Road to Emmaus
Session 1

Welcome and Introductions
Group Covenant

Sharing—We covenant to give each person time to share. We will hold each other accountable to stay within time limits of sharing.

Confidentiality—We covenant to respect the confidentiality of other group members. Personal information shared here will stay here.

Attendance—We covenant to make the group a priority in our lives.

Homework—We covenant to read the assigned segments of *On the Road to Emmaus*. Journaling is encouraged, as led by the questions in each section.

Feelings—We will welcome all feelings, including tears, anger, fear, frustration, and confusion. Group members covenant to respect and honor each others' feelings and expression without judgment.

Advice—We will not give advice unless asked! We will listen with compassion.

Uniqueness—We will not compare our grief journeys. Each one is unique!

Sharing

What has brought you to this group? (Members will each take two to three minutes to introduce their loss.)

Travelogue

Introduction to Emmaus
    The story from Luke

The road to Emmaus for us:
  Two levels to experience
  —To understand who Jesus is and embrace his life
  —To understand what Jesus is doing in the midst of
    our grief and embrace it

Focus Verses

John 11:31-36

> *The Jews who were with her in the house, consoling her, saw Mary get up quickly and go out. They followed her because they thought that she was going to the tomb to weep there. When Mary came where Jesus was and saw him, she knelt at his feet and said to him, "Lord, if you had been here, my brother would not have died." When Jesus saw her weeping, and the Jews who came with her also weeping, he was greatly disturbed in spirit and deeply moved. He said, "Where have you laid him?" They said to him, "Lord, come and see." Jesus began to weep. So the Jews said, "See how much he loved him!"*

Meditation and Reflection: We will observe a few moments of silent meditation after the reading and then welcome members' comments.

Concluding Prayer

How can we pray for one another today? We will go around the circle, so that those who wish to voice a prayer request can do so. Then the facilitator will offer the prayer to God.

Assignment

Read Part One of *On the Road to Emmaus*. Try reading one segment each day. Allow half an hour or more to read, contemplate, journal, and pray.

Next week, consider bringing a picture of the loved one whose loss has brought you to this group.

Bring your copy of *On the Road to Emmaus* to each group session.

Companions on the Road to Emmaus
Session 2

Reflections or Questions on the Reading
Sharing

Those who want to can show a picture of the loved one they lost and share about their relationship with this person.

Travelogue

Reality bytes.

Focus Verses

2 Corinthians 4:7-11

> *But we have this treasure in clay jars, so that it may be made clear that this extraordinary power belongs to God and does not come from us. We are afflicted in every way, but not crushed; perplexed, but not driven to despair; persecuted, but not forsaken; struck down, but not destroyed; always carrying in the body the death of Jesus, so that the life of Jesus may be made visible in our mortal flesh.*

Serenity Prayer: See page 13 in *On the Road to Emmaus*.

Meditation and Reflection: We will observe a few moments of silent meditation after the reading, and then welcome members' comments.

Concluding Prayer

How can we pray for one another today? We will go around the circle so that those who wish to voice a prayer request can do so. Then the facilitator will offer the prayer to God.

Assignment

Read Part Two of *On the Road to Emmaus*.

Companions on the Road to Emmaus
Session 3

Reflections or Questions on the Reading
Travelogue

Learning to grieve.

Sharing

How did you learn to grieve? Is there anything you need to *unlearn*?

What are some non-material things that your loved one gave you that you will continue to treasure throughout your life (for instance, Ed gave me a love of fly fishing).

Focus Verses

Matthew 5:4
> *Blessed are those who mourn, for they will be comforted.*

Isaiah 55:8-11
> *For my thoughts are not your thoughts, nor are your ways my ways, says the LORD. For as the heavens are higher than the earth, so are my ways higher than your ways and my thoughts than your thoughts. For as the rain and the snow come down from heaven, and do not return there until they have watered the earth, making it bring forth and sprout, giving seed to the sower and bread to the eater, so shall my word be that goes out from my mouth; it shall not return to me empty, but it shall accomplish that which I purpose, and succeed in the thing for which I sent it.*

"Holy Darkness" (see pages 50–51)

Meditation and Reflection: We will observe a few moments of silent meditation after the reading and then welcome members' comments.

Concluding Prayer

How can we pray for one another today? We will go around the circle, so that those who wish to voice a prayer request can do so. Then the facilitator will offer the prayer to God.

Assignment

Read Part Three of *On the Road to Emmaus.*

Next week bring an item of memorabilia, something that you have kept because it belonged to your loved one, or because it reminds you of him/her.

Companions on the Road to Emmaus
Session 4

Reflections or Questions on the Reading
Travelogue

Tasks to be accomplished on the road to Emmaus:

- Embrace the loss.
- Reorganize your life.
- Live into God's future.

Sharing

Talk about the item that you brought that is reminiscent of your loved one.

Who are some of the strangers you have met along the road who have helped you in your grief? What characteristics have made these people special? (Do they know how special they are to you?)

Focus Verses

Psalm 23

The LORD is my shepherd, I shall not want.
He makes me lie down in green pastures;
he leads me beside still waters;
he restores my soul.
He leads me in right paths
for his name's sake.

Even though I walk through the darkest valley,
I fear no evil;
for you are with me;
your rod and your staff—
they comfort me.

You prepare a table before me
   in the presence of my enemies;
you anoint my head with oil;
   my cup overflows.
Surely goodness and mercy shall follow me
   all the days of my life,
and I shall dwell in the house of the LORD
   my whole life long.

Patient Trust: See pages 76–77 in *On the Road to Emmaus.*

Meditation and Reflection: We will observe a few moments of silent meditation after the reading, and then welcome comments.

Concluding Prayer

How can we pray for one another today? We will go around the circle, and those who wish to voice a prayer request may do so. Then the facilitator will offer the prayer to God.

Assignment

Read Part Four of *On the Road to Emmaus.*

Companions on the Road to Emmaus
Session 5

Reflections or Questions on the Reading
Sharing

Share your answers to one or more of these questions:

- How do you feel about being a survivor?
- What's something that you have to do now because your loved one is not here to do it for you?
- What strengths or abilities have you discovered in yourself since your loved one died?
- Where have you experienced hope recently?

Travelogue

The light at the end of the tunnel.

Focus Verses

Romans 5:1-5

Therefore, since we are justified by faith, we have peace with God through our Lord Jesus Christ, through whom we have obtained access to this grace in which we stand; and we boast in our hope of sharing the glory of God. And not only that, but we also boast in our sufferings, knowing that suffering produces endurance, and endurance produces character, and character produces hope, and hope does not disappoint us, because God's love has been poured into our hearts through the Holy Spirit that has been given to us.

Meditation and Reflection: We will observe a few moments of silent meditation after the reading, and then welcome members' comments.

Concluding Prayer

How can we pray for one another today? We will go around the circle so that those who wish to voice a prayer request can do so. Then the facilitator will offer the prayer to God

Assignment

Read Part Five of *On the Road to Emmaus.*

Think about where you want to go from here. Next week is our last scheduled session. Are you ready to move away from the group, or would you like more sessions?

Companions on the Road to Emmaus
Session 6

Reflections or Questions on the Reading

Answer this question: When you think about Emmaus, what does it "look like"?

Travelogue

I left my heart in Emmaus.

Sharing

Take a few moments to consider our time together, your reading and meditating, and your journey to Emmaus and beyond. Review the questions on the last two pages of your reading assignment.

Also consider again the three tasks (turns) in the road to Emmaus:

- Embrace your grief.

- Reorganize your life.

- Live into God's future.

Tell us your story again, this time emphasizing where you are now in relation to Emmaus. Are you still on your way to Emmaus? Have you been there and back again? (What did you discover there?) What do you still need?

Focus Verses

2 Corinthians 1:3-11

Blessed be the God and Father of our Lord Jesus Christ, the Father of mercies and the God of all consolation, who consoles us in all our affliction, so that we may be able to console those who are in any affliction with the consolation with which we ourselves are consoled by God. For just as the sufferings of Christ are abundant for us, so also our consolation is abundant through Christ. If we are being afflicted, it is for your consolation and salvation; if we are being consoled, it is for your consolation, which you experience when you patiently endure the same sufferings that we are also suffering. Our hope for you is unshaken; for we know that as you share in our sufferings, so also you share in our consolation.

We do not want you to be unaware, brothers and sisters, of the affliction we experienced in Asia; for we were so utterly, unbearably crushed that we despaired of life itself. Indeed, we felt that we had received the sentence of death so that we would rely not on ourselves but on God who raises the dead. He who rescued us from so deadly a peril will continue to rescue us; on him we have set our hope that he will rescue us again, as you also join in helping us by your prayers, so that many will give thanks on our behalf for the blessing granted us through the prayers of many.

Meditation and Reflection: We will observe a few moments of silent meditation after the reading, and then welcome members' comments.

Concluding Prayer

How can we pray for one another today? We will go around the circle so that those who wish to voice a prayer request can do so. Then the facilitator will offer the prayer to God.

Assignment

Continue your journey! As we close today, we ask whether any participants wish to continue on in the group after today's session.